AF304912

MUD PIES AND TALL TOWERS

MUD PIES AND TALL TOWERS

Playful Mathematics activities for the under 5s

Helen J. Williams

S Sage

3rd Floor
HYLO
103–105 Bunhill Row
London, EC1Y 8LZ
UK

2455 Teller Road
Thousand Oaks
California 91320

10th Floor, Emaar Capital Tower
2 MG Road, Sikanderpur, Sector 26
Gurugram, Haryana – 122002
India

8 Marina View Suite 43–053
Asia Square Tower 1
Singapore 018960

Editor: Amy Thornton
Production editor: Imogen Roome
Copyeditor: Sarah Bury
Marketing manager: Dilhara Attygalle
Cover design: Sheila Tong
Typeset by: C&M Digitals (P) Ltd, Chennai, India
Printed in the UK by Bell and Bain Ltd, Glasgow
BB0365495

© Helen J. Williams 2026

Apart from any fair dealing for the purposes of research, private study, or criticism or review, as permitted under the Copyright, Designs and Patents Act, 1988, this publication may not be reproduced, stored or transmitted in any form, or by any means, without the prior permission in writing of the publisher, or in the case of reprographic reproduction, in accordance with the terms of licences issued by the Copyright Licensing Agency. Enquiries concerning reproduction outside those terms should be sent to the publisher.

No AI training. Without in any way limiting the author's and publisher's exclusive rights under copyright, any use of this publication to `train' generative artificial intelligence (AI) or for other AI uses is expressly prohibited. The publisher reserves all rights to license uses of this publication for generative AI training or other AI uses.

Library of Congress Control Number available

British Library Cataloguing in Publication data

A catalogue record for this book is available from the British Library

ISBN 978-1-5296-8975-4
ISBN 978-1-5296-8974-7 (pbk)

This book is dedicated to Mike Ollerton, my wonderful ATM colleague over many years.

CONTENTS

LIST OF TASKS

ABOUT THE AUTHOR

Dr Helen J. Williams has worked for many years in education and is an independent consultant specialising in the learning and teaching of early mathematics. Her work has included researching and writing about mathematics education, teaching alongside colleagues in schools and settings, as well as contributing to ITT and in-service conferences across the UK and Europe. In 2024 she was awarded lifetime membership of the Association of Teachers of Mathematics for whom she has written materials and run conference sessions over many years. She is a member of the British Society for Research into Learning Mathematics (https://bsrlm.org.uk), an associate of Early Education (https://early-education.org.uk) and an active member of the Early Childhood Mathematics Group (ECMG) (https://earlymaths.org), a UK-based group of mathematics enthusiasts and experts who work together to promote a better understanding of mathematics from birth to 8 years and produce free, high-quality, research-informed guidance and materials for all those involved in early years education.

Helen's doctorate was completed with the University of Roehampton, London, in 2014 and explored the mathematical potential of role play in Reception and Year 4.

She posts on Bluesky as @helenjwc.bsky.social and blogs (sporadically) here: https://info125328.wixsite.com/website.

Helen's book *Playful Mathematics for Children 3 to 7* was published by SAGE in March 2022 and later that year won the Nursery World Professional Book of the Year (https://us.sagepub.com/en-us/nam/playful-mathematics/book276080).

Helen became a mathematics enthusiast only after teaching her first Reception class in the 1980s and pondering what sense these 4- and 5-year-olds were making of what she offered them.

ACKNOWLEDGEMENTS

Thank you in bucketfuls to the wonderful, insightful practitioners who tried things out, took photographs and provided feedback – in particular, Maeve Birdsall and Esther O'Connor – as well as to my amazing colleagues in the Early Childhood Mathematics Group for many stimulating discussions and their invaluable feedback on early drafts.

A very special thank you to the children, families and staff of the following settings for bringing these activities alive with their images: The British School of Brussels, Manor Wood Primary School Leeds and Tadcaster Primary Academy.

In her innovative 1976 book *Mathematics Their Way*, Mary Baratta-Lorton has this dedication, which I reproduce in part here:

To children, lost in a world of adult symbols which they cannot begin to fathom

And

To teachers, lost in a world of methods and materials they did not create and in which they no longer have faith.

Here's to a better way that evolves when we look at learning their way.

Figure 1.0 Pattern making

1

AN INTRODUCTION

A society without mathematical affection is like a city without concerts, parks or museums.

(Su 2020: 8)

Over the last 30 or more years, I have worked to connect two things that I love, mathematics learning and teaching, with working with young children. I did not always love mathematics, but I have always found it fascinating to work mathematically with children of all ages. *What are they making of this? Why aren't they interested? How can I make this task more engaging for them?*

Recently, with a friend and her 11-month-old grandson, I attended a 'Rhyme Time' session for babies and toddlers at the local library. The person running the session was engaging and inventive, and all of the 20 or so toddlers and babies were absorbed for an hour, clapping, laughing, moving, joining in and simply gazing. As I watched her introduce a helium balloon and allow it to rise up to the high ceiling, with the children practically holding their communal breath, it struck me what a lovely opportunity it was to play with some mathematical ideas: *I wonder, will it touch the ceiling? What if I let go of the string? Can I still reach the string if I do let it go? How tall do I need to be? What if I can't reach it?* Actually, the play leader had underestimated the amount of string needed, culminating in them having to fetch first a stool and then a stepladder to retrieve it. Every one of these very young children was fascinated by the whole episode and those who were older were making suggestions about how to reach it. Many events present the opportunity for mathematical discussions with our youngest children. On the way home from playgroup, the church clock strikes.

Alice (3 years old):	Clock donging! … one … two … three … [continues counting and reaches 11].
Adult:	Wow! How many dongs was that?
	[Alice doesn't answer.]

In this book you will find ideas to enhance our youngest children's life experiences, language and, in particular, their learning and confidence in mathematics. I hope they also enhance your experience of mathematics. I have written ideas as activities to undertake together, but there are so many mathematical possibilities in everyday events, such as the above example. Having tried some of these, I hope you are also able to spot these opportunities out and about in your own 'everyday'. The balloon episode is written up as 'Balloon rising' in Chapter Four, which is focused on the area of measures (see page 95).

I have aimed this book at those of us working and living with children under 5 years of age, but many of the ideas and activities can be adapted for older children. It is a companion book to my book, *Playful Mathematics for Children 3 to 7* (Williams 2022).

This book comprises an introduction and a conclusion, which bookend three chapters of activities that have been organised under these broad mathematical areas:

- Chapter Two: Mainly Shape and Space (otherwise known as geometry)
- Chapter Three: Mainly Number and Pattern
- Chapter Four: Mainly Measures.

You will notice that neither mathematics nor the children's activity slots neatly into one area, and there is much overlap between the activities. At the front of the book there is an alphabetical list of named tasks, along with the page number, to help you find, and repeat, yours and your children's favourite activities. Repetition – or as I prefer to call it, *re-visiting* – is as important in mathematics as in any other area. Children gain much from hearing the same story over and over, and this is also true of mathematical activities and games. Returning to something builds familiarity, providing children with opportunities to build on what they already know, and make connections between older and newer learning. Familiarity brings with it possibilities to reflect on and discuss what is happening, as well as what might happen, all important mathematical thinking experiences. I encourage you and your children to find your own favourites in here and repeat them over and over.

Each chapter contains around 14 ideas for some mathematical play to engage in together (the '***Tasks***'), organised under subheadings for younger and older under-5s, and between those based outdoors and others indoors. None requires specialist equipment and each includes information on the mathematical development behind the task ('***The maths***'), as well as guidance on supporting children's thinking ('***What we do and say***'), together with suggestions for developing the task ('***Broadening this out***' and '***Stories and rhymes***').

Each chapter begins with an easily accessible, short background on the relevant mathematical area ('***About this area of maths*** and '***Why it is important***'). It includes relevant further reading and useful, free, online resources for educators and carers. I make particular mention of the Early Childhood Mathematics Group, of which I am a member, and which have a free and thorough website of guidance and resources for all adults working with children from birth to 8 years of age (https://earlymaths.org).

I often hear people self-report as being underconfident mathematically and it can lead to anxiety when teaching mathematics. We can worry we are 'getting it wrong'. However, it is important that we all – educators, families and carers – demonstrate a positive attitude to mathematics to all children, so that they grow up mathematically confident and curious. We can do this by building our understanding of early mathematics and by being more playful in how we interact mathematically with all our children. These two threads are at the heart of this book. Research by Dowker and her colleagues (2019) into relationships between children's attitude to mathematics at age 5–6 (in their first year of statutory schooling in the UK) suggests that, even at this young age, attitudes to mathematics are associated with performance; how children feel about themselves and mathematics lies at the core of their attitude to the subject (Dowker et al. 2019). Those of us who work and live with toddlers and young children have a crucial role to play here:

> *Creating fearless learning environments that allow for failure, and that enable children to make early experiences of success, is an important challenge for early mathematics education.*
>
> (Obersteiner 2019: 321)

Play-like situations can help to establish a fearless learning environment. Playing mathematically helps to develop mathematical curiosity, creativity and imagination.

PLAY AND PLAYFULNESS

Figure 1.1   Play: Printing rings

Play is fundamentally important for children. It is by playing that they learn. Play is intrinsically motivating. It is memorable and mindful. We can use play to make mathematics more in touch with the children we work with, providing a space where they can build on their prior experiences. The word 'play' encompasses such a wide assortment of activities, from private and imaginative to public performances, that I choose to use the word '*playful*'. This word recognises that whoever initiates the task, adult or child, it is what happens after that introduction that is important. Being playful combines play and guidance. We can use the motivation and creativity that children bring to their free play with a Vygotskian recognition that children's learning can be expanded when sensitively supported by an adult (Vygotsky 1966). Skene and her colleagues refer to this process as '*guided play*' (Skene *et al.* 2022). These authors' meta-analysis of research into effective play identify three important characteristics of guided play:

- Sensitive adult guidance
- A learning goal or intention
- Child autonomy, where tasks and interactions include time for children to take a lead in what happens mathematically.

I find that the last characteristic is what is missing from most mathematical interactions, so the tasks in this book include the space for child autonomy to take place.

Being playful is also key to the *Characteristics of Teaching and Learning*, an essential element of the statutory Early Years Foundation Stage in England (Department for Education 2024a, 2024b). These apply to mathematics as much as to any other area of learning. The three Characteristics of Teaching and Learning are:

- **Playing and exploring** – Children investigate and experience things, and 'have a go'
- **Active learning** – Children concentrate and keep on trying if they encounter difficulties, and enjoy achievements
- **Creating and thinking critically** – Children have and develop their own ideas, make links between ideas and develop strategies for doing things.

(Department for Education 2024a: 17, 2024b: 12)

You will find that these characteristics are integrated into suggestions for '**What we do and say**', as well as how the tasks are initially introduced.

Play is not only for younger children. Francis Su is professor of mathematics at Harvey Mudd College, California, and in his 2020 book, *Mathematics for Human Flourishing*, he argues that mathematical play builds curiosity, confidence, concentration, perseverance and patience:

> *Play is fundamental to who we are as human beings, and the desire for play can entice everyone to do and enjoy, mathematics.*

(Su 2020: 64)

WHAT IS MATHEMATICS?

Figure 1.2   Mathematics: Recording amounts

Math is intimately tied to being human.

(Su 2020: x)

So writes mathematician Francis Su, and yet this is not the sense many of us have had of school mathematics. Instead, we might have been more worried about failure and how we performed in relation to our peers. Concern about performance makes it difficult for us to enjoy exploring mathematically. And yet, when we observe our youngest children, so much of what they do displays behaviours that are crucial for doing mathematics. This list is an amalgam of many who have discussed significant mathematical behaviours, such as Cuoco et al. (1996) and Mason et al. (2010):

- Exploring and experimenting
- Imagining
- Expressing and communicating
- Specialising
- Classifying and organising
- Predicting and conjecturing
- Convincing
- Reflecting
- Extending
- Generalising.

Below is one example of how these behaviours might be observed in young children's play:

Figure 1.3 Building a block house

Outdoors, playing with a selection of bricks and blocks two 3-year-olds are selecting blocks and putting them on one of two broad towers, separated by a space. They spend some time looking for a long enough plank to successfully bridge the two towers, discarding some and trying others until they are happy. They can be heard using words like 'door', 'wall' and 'big' and seem to be collaborating to build a house.

Here we can see children *exploring* the shapes of the bricks and *experimenting* to build something they have *imagined* and *expressed* to each other. They *organise* their play, *communicate* some of their thoughts and are observed *predicting* which plank will reach across the space they have made. With sensitive adult input, they could be encouraged to *convince* us they have chosen the correct plank (*"Is this one any good for this?"*) and to *reflect* on their construction (*"Is the doorway high enough for you to fit under?"*) and even to *extend* their ideas (*"Where might you build your bedroom?"*).

Mathematics pervades every aspect of life and is internationally valued by educators, employers and the public alike. The definition of mathematics has been reconceptualised over time as new branches of mathematics have been developed. Broadly speaking, mathematics is a socially constructed, symbolic language used to represent relationships of number and of geometry and to convey these ideas to others. Mathematics consists of a collection of mathematical content (geometry, pattern, number, etc.) and a set of logical processes (symbolising, problem-solving, generalising, etc.). We can think of mathematics in relation to very young children as noticing the properties of, and relationships between, numbers, sizes, shapes etc., conveying these ideas to others – children and adults – and representing these in different ways, through talk, gesture and graphics. Figure 1.4 is the recording of two 4-year-olds keeping scores in a game, as they symbolise effectively what is happening as their game progresses.

Here are eight principles for appropriate early mathematics:

1. All children are entitled to be mathematical and learn mathematics.
2. Mathematical development involves learning mathematical behaviours (or ways of working mathematically) as well as mathematical concepts.
3. Young children are differently experienced and not differently able at mathematics.
4. Children are entitled to pedagogy that supports the full breadth of mathematical learning.
5. Early mathematics practice should be shaped by practitioner knowledge of the typical developmental trajectories in mathematics.
6. Young children learn mathematics through play and need time to: (i) follow and develop their own choices and ideas, (ii) play and interact with adults, and (iii) participate in adult-led episodes.
7. Practitioners provide opportunities for mathematical learning through the environment and continuous provision.
8. Children need to have a repertoire of ways in which to communicate their mathematical thinking.

(Gripton and Williams 2023)

It is important to remember that no child is a mathematical blank slate; every child operates mathematically as they negotiate their environment, experience 'environmental' mathematics through packaging, signs and labels, as well as being exposed to 'everyday' mathematical decisions when eating, drinking, playing and moving around. From birth, children explore their surroundings to make sense of them. How we approach mathematics with our youngest children is as important as the mathematical content we introduce. Our job is to support children to see themselves as competent and able to recognise mathematical

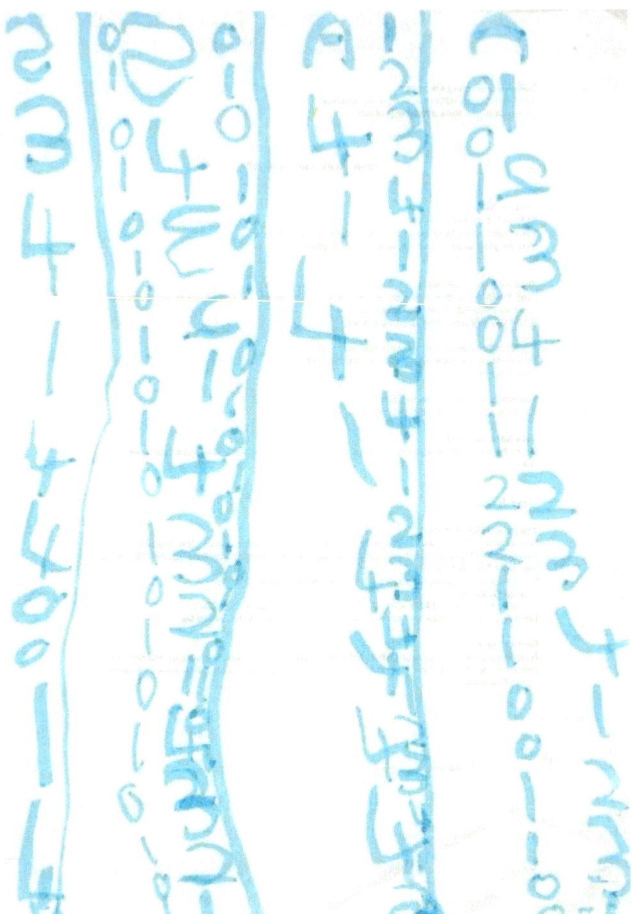

Figure 1.4 Scoring a game

situations (e.g. *"Look how small Gran looks when she's far away!"*) as well as to sensitively mathematise elements of their play to introduce them to new mathematical experiences. I have come to believe there are two main ways to achieve this:

- Play that lends itself to doing something mathematical – sensitively taking advantage of mathematical opportunities within children's play
- Mathematical situations that we make playful, where the child has control and can explore their own curiosities.

Both are effective, and both require the adult to be sympathetic to the child's interests and be prepared to adapt to follow these. The younger the child, the more important it is to adapt to them:

… toddlers' play should be the central focus when teachers are working with mathematics in toddler groups.

(Reikeras 2020: 12)

Reikeras's (2020) research indicates a relatively strong relationship between the level of play skills and the level of mathematical skills among toddlers, particularly their *interaction* and *independence,* and thus the importance of strengthening these skills. She highlights pretend play and exploratory and construction play, rather than rule-based play, as being more suitable for these younger children in connecting them with mathematics.

In the chapters that follow, I outline ideas that I have found to be successful, how to recognise the mathematics in these, and how we might work alongside children to build their ability to interact mathematically with others and with ideas, as well as to nurture their independence. At the root of this approach is us sustaining a mathematical conversation with our children, a to-ing and fro-ing of ideas, trying to make sense of what each of us notices, rather than us telling them what they 'should' be seeing or doing. I think one important role we have as educators of mathematics is one of *guided participation.*

Throughout this book, you will find some activities more suitable for your younger children than others, I have attempted to organise them with this in mind. There is a lot of mathematical development between birth and 4 years of age! It is important to dwell on – and wallow in – our favourite activities rather than 'pushing on'.

HOW TO USE THIS BOOK

First, have a flick through and see if anything takes your fancy or strikes you when thinking about your child(ren). Become familiar with the organisation of the book under three broad mathematical areas: *shape and space, number and pattern* and *measures.* I do not intend that you approach all the number tasks (or measures, or shape and space tasks) at one time, or in one sort of order. That is best decided by you. You may think that focusing on number is more important than any other area, but in fact research is clear that it is *spatial thinking* that is indicative of future and broader mathematical achievement and success (Cheng and Mix 2014; Clements and Sarama 2021; Verdine et al. 2017), and as spatial thinking is an area that has to date been under-prioritised in UK education (Farran et al. 2024), you may prefer to begin here.

Read through a few tasks and the paragraphs on the underlying mathematics. Think about what your children are interested in or ponder something that may capture their interest, and start there. Each task includes some things to say to the children, but it is important that we say nothing to begin with, and instead observe the children's initial reactions, listening to, responding and narrating on these comments only when appropriate. You may choose not to follow the suggested course of the specific idea, and that is fine. The important thing is to work, play, chat and think mathematically together, and to show genuine interest in what the children say and do, e.g. *"I see you are making that tower taller and taller!"* This approach allows time to engage in some *'sustained shared thinking'* (Sylva et al. 2004) and *'exploratory talk'* (Mercer and Hodgkinson 2008), both of which have been found to be important for children's learning. Time to wallow with the resources, building

Figure 1.5 Three under the cups

interest and familiarity, is important, providing opportunities to introduce new language and vocabulary.

FINALLY

I hope this book supports you in both recognising and affirming to others that we do not need a published mathematics scheme or structured 'numeracy' programme with children in this age group. It is perfectly possible, and far preferable, to cover important mathematical ideas that are tied into our and our children's natural interests and curiosities. Published schemes are not aware of your children, their development or their interests; they do not prioritise children's curiosity or positive attitudes and are only suitable for much older children, and even then, they should not provide their whole mathematical diet. As our knowledge of early mathematics and children's mathematical development grows, we can confidently ask ourselves "where are the mathematical opportunities … here … and here … today?".

I end this chapter with a lovely extract to reflect on, written by the American author, educator and *kindergarten teacher, Vivian Gussin Paley:*

Wally:	People don't feel the same as grown-ups.
Teacher:	Do you mean "Children don't"?
Wally:	Because grown-ups don't remember when they were little. They're already an old person. Only if you have a picture of you doing that. Then you could remember.
Eddie:	But not thinking.
Wally:	You never can take a picture of thinking. Of course not.

(Gussin Paley 1981: 4)

I hope that, within this collection of mathematical ideas for carers and children to experience (and re-visit), you begin to remember what it is to be little and to discover something for the first time, and that you find many mathematical moments to enjoy together.

Figure 2.0   Block construction

2

MAINLY SHAPE AND SPACE

Countries improving spatial skills will "mean that their citizens are better prepared for everyday life in our rapidly changing technological society."

(Sorby and Panther 2020: 230).

"Teaching of geometry cannot be only about enhancing a child's knowledge and skills, but should also focus on the child's dispositions and feelings"

(Dindyal 2015: 525).

SECTION 1 – ABOUT THIS AREA OF MATHS

The area of mathematics often referred to as 'shape and space', otherwise known as 'geometry', consists of the following:

- ***Shape* understanding** – the *properties* of objects and shapes (both two-dimensional, or flat, and three-dimensional) and how they are constructed (e.g. they roll, are pointy, or circular, they fit together to make this new shape). Although shape understanding does involve learning the different names for shapes, this element is only one very small part of this area of mathematics.
- ***Spatial* understanding** – *location*: where things – including ourselves – are positioned and where they are in relation to other things (behind, on top, far away, this way up etc.) *along with direction*, how and where to move and navigate.

Learning about these two areas interrelates and overlaps. *Spatial reasoning* is something we all use continually in our everyday lives, for example when parking the car, packing bags, finding our way around, and so on. To *reason spatially,* we make decisions based on our understandings of the properties of shapes, position and direction. Understanding maps, diagrams and two-dimensional images of our three-dimensional world are all important for spatial reasoning.

Over time, children gradually progress from awareness and recognition of different shapes and their interactions with the world spatially, through visualising and representing verbally and graphically (e.g. talking about what they see, or drawing a route), to predicting and reasoning. The development of spatial reasoning is dependent on much practical experience, both indoors and outside. Physical activity is very important, with plenty of time for babies to explore the spatial relationships between body parts, such as feet and hands, to crawl, to distinguish between shapes and objects, and later, opportunities for toddlers to explore and discuss different places outdoors, finding their way from place to place, fitting themselves and other items into spaces and looking from different viewpoints. The activities in this chapter are designed to provide important experiences like these.

You will find some activities more suitable for your younger children than others. There is much mathematical development between the ages of 18 months and 4 years. It is important to dwell on – and wallow in – our favourite activities rather than 'pushing on'. Providing time to play with spatial toys, such as posting-shape boxes, jigsaws, boxes of different objects to feel, blocks, Duplo, stacking cups, etc. is important in developing children's thinking and visualisation. If you have a limited budget, many of these toys can be found in charity shops.

WHY IT IS IMPORTANT

There is overwhelming evidence of the link between being able to reason spatially and wider, later achievement in mathematics, as well as links to understanding science, technology and the arts (Gifford et al. 2022; Gilligan et al. 2019; Pritulsky et al. 2020). Even young children's ability to think and reason spatially can be developed by adults in playful ways (Uttal et al. 2013).

Babies' spatial development begins by them becoming aware of distinctions between shapes and objects (what is a teddy and what is a ball, for example) and their awareness of space and distance (when reaching for a toy, or recognising a familiar person far away, for example). Spatial reasoning also involves interpreting images and diagrams and relating these to real life. While many of us have tackled assembling flat-pack furniture, very young children begin by relating a picture of a car to one outside on the road, or recognising images and drawings of familiar items from different perspectives, for example. Going out and about together, even locally, and talking through these journeys is valuable in building a rich store of spatial experiences relating to distance and direction. Providing photographs of familiar as well as unfamiliar places to discuss enriches the experience, as do unusual images of familiar objects to chat about. We can support children's development by introducing new spatial language, alongside hand gestures, to help children to understand what more unfamiliar words mean, such as: 'beneath', or 'between', or 'flip'.

FURTHER READING

The UK-based Early Childhood Mathematics Group of early years' mathematics enthusiasts and experts has a significant section of their website dedicated to the understanding of the learning and teaching of shape and space, alongside resources for practitioners. All their materials are freely available at: https://earlymaths.org/spatial-reasoning/

Gifford, S., Gripton, C., Williams, H. J., Lancaster, A., Bates, K. E., Williams, A. Y., Gilligan-Lee, K., Borthwick, A., & Farran, E. K. (2022). *Spatial reasoning in early childhood.* https://psyarxiv.com/jnwpu/download?format=pdf

Gilligan, K. A., Hodgkiss, A., Thomas, M. S., & Farran, E. K. (2019). The developmental relations between spatial cognition and mathematics in primary school children. *Developmental Science, 22*(4). https://doi.org/10.1111/desc.12786

Information on self-regulation can be found in this freely available resource (important for changing perspective): https://birthto5matters.org.uk/self-regulation/

SECTION 2 – TASKS

The following tasks explore shape and space.

OUTDOOR TASKS FOR YOUNGER CHILDREN

TASK: OBSTACLE COURSE; OVER, ALONG AND THROUGH

Figure 2.1   Obstacle course

PROVIDE

A selection of 'obstacles' from large loose parts (e.g. crates, boxes, planks, bricks, chairs, blankets, tyres) and playground chalks for children to co-create their own obstacle course. They are given plenty of time to play on it.

THE MATHS

This task mainly develops children's *spatial* awareness. Physical development is at the core of children's understanding of spatial relations. They learn about *direction* and how we navigate around, including our *distance* and *position* in relation to other objects, as well as how things look from different positions. To enrich children's spatial language and vocabulary, adults can describe the movements children make as they navigate the obstacles, encouraging children to do the same, e.g. *over, under, through, between, higher, behind, before, first, next...*, and so on.

WHAT WE DO AND SAY

I can see you like balancing along the planks.

I see you're going to start at the tyre and go forwards ... you have jumped in that circle. Where next, I wonder?

I think we can build something for someone to go underneath.

Ooo that looks tricky!

So high you can't go OVER it... so low you can't go UNDER it ... so wide you can't go ROUND it ... you gotta go THROUGH it!

BROADENING THIS OUT

- After they have enjoyed all the balancing and crawling for a while, you can encourage children to consider starting in different places, with you narrating their different routes through the obstacles: "First you are walking along ..., then you go under the ...". Children may like to plot a route from a 'START' to a 'FINISH' marked on the ground.
- Invite the child to follow a route that you call out, emphasising positional and directional language by using hand gestures: "Can you go up the steps and under the blanket?", "Through the tunnel, along the plank ...?"
- Invite a child to narrate or sing their journey: "Can you say what you are doing as you go along?" For example, "I am going over, I am going through ...".
- Read together *We're Going on a Bear Hunt*, by Michael Rosen, and watch his performance at: www.youtube.com/watch?v=0gyl6ykDwds

TASK: WALK AND TALK

Figure 2.2   Walk and talk

PROVIDE

A safe, familiar space for a walk. Make sure there are plenty of adults!

THE MATHS

Going out and about develops children's *spatial* awareness of direction and position. Learning about direction and how we navigate around is part of children's understanding of spatial relations. Talking about where we are going and using gestures associated with the directional words we use (*"Straight along this road/path"*, *"We turn left at the corner ahead"*, *"Round the flower bed"*, *"Stop in front of the sign"*) helps children to understand these directional and positional words. Their awareness of their surroundings, starting from the familiar, which they are more likely to talk about, can lead to wider awareness and discussions about maps, distances (relatively how near and how far) and even time (how long a journey takes).

WHAT WE DO AND SAY

The chat can start before we leave base or, with younger children, when we arrive at the starting point of the walk and before we set off.

Provide a photograph of the starting point: *Do you know this place? Tell me about it.*

Have you been here before? It is quite near your home, Isaac, so you might have walked here.
Off we go. We turn left up here, don't we?
Which way now?

BROADENING THIS OUT

- The benefit of this activity is in doing it often – in the same place as well as in different places – to build children's confidence and language. Can they find the route or a landmark from last time? Gradually, if undertaken in a familiar park, for example, children might find their own routes to navigate.
- A strip of card prepared with a line of double-sided tape can become a child's 'collecting card', where they choose found items along the walk to remember where they went. Collecting in a bag means they must order the items when they tip them out.
- When appropriate, with older children, introduce clipboards and a pen for them to record landmarks as they go. It is important they choose their landmarks and do their own recording. These can provide the provocation for discussions on return.
- Creating a 'Map of where I live'. Provide pens and large sheets of blank paper and invite children to make their own maps to talk about.
- Walk a play-person through a route and narrate their journey.

Figure 2.3 Drawing a map

- Hide some 'treasure' and tell a friend how to find it or draw a treasure map for someone to follow to find it.

TASK: HIDING AND PEEPING

Figure 2.4   Hiding and peeping

PROVIDE

Large boxes, curtains, an indoor or outside area with obstacles large enough to hide behind/under.

Play hide and seek. Encourage the finder to *say where* the hider was hiding.

THE MATHS

We have all experienced toddlers covering just their eyes when asked to hide, in the belief that if they cannot see, no one can see them. This is because hide and seek depends on a child's ability to change *perspective* and be aware that others may have a different viewpoint from them. This awareness is quite sophisticated and takes time to develop, but appreciating perspective is an important part of wider mathematical understanding. Hide and seek also requires a lot of self-control; that is *self-regulation*, in order not to call out and give the hiding place away! If they do call out, we can still chat about where they were.

This activity also focuses on responding to and understanding the language and vocabulary of position: *under the blanket*, *behind the tree*, etc. Gradually, we want children to begin to use these words.

WHAT WE DO AND SAY

No peeping out! I'll stay still here until you're really hidden.

Can you think of a place to hide, really well, from me?

Let's go and find some good hiding places together. Then you can secretly choose one.

Can you say where Leah was hiding?

BROADENING THIS OUT

- Give a secret instruction to a child to hide somewhere specific: *"I'd like you to hide under the slide."*
- While playing with small world and block/construction, introduce two playpeople, position one at the edge of the construction and invite children to hide the other one from the first figure: *"Are they hiding well, there?".*
- Introduce some long card tubes and invite children to look into them to find some familiar – and not so familiar – objects (e.g. our climbing frame, or a tree). Then someone can go and stand by it.
- Read *Everyone Hide from Wibbly Pig,* by Mick Inkpen: www.youtube.com/watch?v=-pSYdNDmmdk

OUTDOOR TASKS FOR OLDER, MORE EXPERIENCED CHILDREN

TASK: MY MAP

PROVIDE

A well-known obstacle course (see the 'Obstacle course' task for younger children at the beginning of this section, p. 16), clipboards and pens or large sheets of paper, playpeople and Duplo bricks.

Co-construct a linear map of the familiar obstacle course, perhaps with agreed symbols or blocks for obstacles and arrows showing a route through.

THE MATHS

There is a progression through creating, doing and talking through an obstacle course, to linking this to a representation, as this involves connecting the memory of physical navigation to a symbolic and scaled spatial representation. Related research points to the following findings:

(Continued)

at around 3 years, children can understand a basic aerial photo of familiar objects, such as toys (Catling 2005) and at around 4 years, children can use a basic map to follow a route. This activity is about children experiencing symbolic representations and beginning to interact with them.

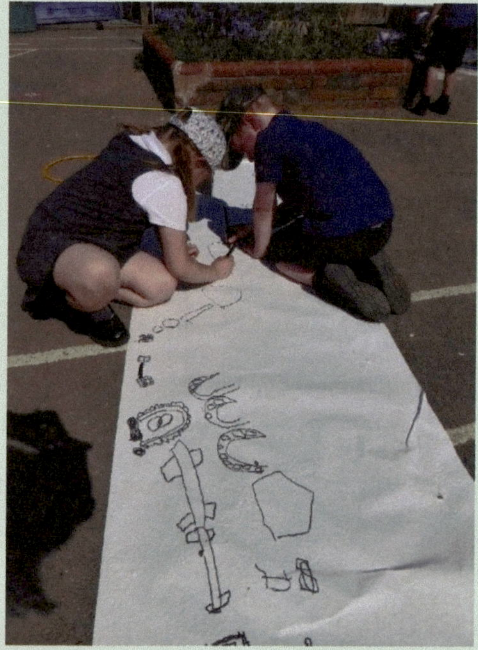

Figure 2.5   Recording an outdoor obstacle course

WHAT WE DO AND SAY

- You can point to an obstacle on their map and ask them to stand at that exact point on the obstacle course. Or switch this around so that they point and you stand in the place on the course. You can try making a 'mistake' and see if they correct you.
- How shall we draw that tyre?
- What comes after the long plank?
- I am going to show a way to go with my finger ... round here, over this ...
- Read *Inside Out, Upside Down*, by Stan and Jan Berenstein: www.youtube.com/watch?v=fAVdDwP2aPO

BROADENING THIS OUT

- Direct friends around their map: over the rope, under the chair, between the blocks ...
- Add some road maps to the block and small-world or road-play area.

- Explore different points of view in a familiar place by finding somewhere to safely hang upside down, or look through something low down or high up.
- Co-create a small-world replica of the obstacle course for the playpeople.
- Co-create a three-dimensional map of their setting or another familiar area using boxes for agreed landmarks. They can play with this, navigating cars and playpeople around while we introduce the directional words, e.g. *straight on, stop at the bridge, turn here...*

TASK: ODD ONE OUT

PROVIDE

Leaves that the children have collected and a tray. Invite the children to point to or pick up one they like. Use the children's own words and informal vocabulary to describe this activity, e.g. *pointy, wide, like a hand, sharp, shiny, huge...*

Choose four leaves and put them on the tray. Ask if someone can point to an 'odd one out'. It is important that the children decide which leaf this is and begin to think about why.

THE MATHS

This task develops children's awareness of the different and similar *properties of shapes* as well as familiarity with the associated language to describe features and positions.

'Which One Doesn't Belong' is a website dedicated to providing similar puzzles for every age of learner. There are no 'right answers' as there are different, equally correct ways of choosing 'which one doesn't belong' (WODB). The eventual goal is for the child to say 'why' an object does not belong in order to explain (or justify) their choice. 'Kim's Game' (see 'Broadening out', below) utilises their working memory. Can they remember what the toothbrush was *next* to, for example? They may need more than one peep to play confidently.

WHAT WE DO AND SAY

What do you like about this one? Maybe how it feels or maybe its size?

Which one do you think is the odd one out?

Can you find me another leaf that is the same as this one? Can you point to another leaf that is spikey like this one?

(Continued)

Can you point to where these leaves are the same?

(Modelling) That's a great odd one out! I think I might choose this one, as it is the only one with a long stalk.

You've chosen two! What can you say about each of them?

BROADENING THIS OUT

- Repeat the task with petals, shells, sticks or pebbles: *What shall we play this with next time?*
- The task can be an indoor activity using familiar toys.
- 'Kim's Game' is an old party game where a few familiar objects are placed on a tray, which is covered after everyone has had a good look at the items. One item is secretly removed, or a change made to the layout on the tray. Can children spot what is missing or what has changed?
- Put together a Treasure Jar for children to tip out and explore. Introduce a group activity where you pass the jar around and choose an item to show and talk about.

TASK: PICNIC

Figure 2.6   Picnic

PROVIDE

A tablecloth, preferably square or rectangular, enough plates and cups for every child to have one each. Something to eat and drink.

Invite the children to come and sit around the 'table'. Encourage them to spread out *along each edge* of the cloth. Discuss who is sitting *next to, beside, in between, opposite* whom. Invite children to give out the plates and cups using positional vocabulary, e.g. *"This one is for Sudip and this one is for the person sitting next to him"*.

THE MATHS

This task is about experiencing and building familiarity with *positional vocabulary*, some of which is easier to understand than others; for example, 'in between' is harder. Adult hand gestures help children to make sense of the words we are using. The younger the child, the more statements we make and the fewer questions we ask.

WHAT WE DO AND SAY

Let's spread out so we're sitting all the way around the outside/edge.

If you stand up, Pip, who can you see next to you / each side of you?

Sudip is next to Pip and Pip is next to Rose ....

Point to who you can see on the opposite side of the picnic cloth.

BROADENING THIS OUT

- This task can be adapted to an indoor activity for just one or two children using dolls and teddies having a picnic.
- Play 'swap places': Call out instructions for the children to follow, e.g. *"Pip, swap with Finn. Now who are you next to?"* Ask children who they want to swap with and to say who they will be next to when they change places.
- Use the home corner to lay the table and get invited to a party where you can have these discussions. Maybe the invitation can say who you will be sitting *next to, opposite* Big Ted, Baby, etc.

TASK: LEAF AND FRUIT SHAPES

Figure 2.7   Fruit shapes drawn

Figure 2.8   Drawing fruit shapes

PROVIDE

Magnifying glasses and a selection of leaves. Alternatively, slices of fruit and/or vegetables. With the children, examine each leaf (piece of fruit or vegetable), chat together about the texture, the shape and the markings. Leave these out along with drawing materials for children to examine in their own time.

On later occasions, cut different fruit and vegetables in half with the children, inviting children to imagine (*predict*) what the vegetable or fruit *may look like* when it is cut open in different ways and examine the shapes inside. Explore putting the halves back together and splitting them apart again.

Figure 2.9   Half a melon

Figure 2.10   Apple halves

THE MATHS

Children's experiences of *shape and pattern* are enriched by observing and exploring natural patterns that occur. Moreover, children can be encouraged to notice and think about *similarities and differences* in these items – an important aspect of mathematics.

Inside vegetables such as a red cabbage or an onion, it is possible to see spirals or rings, and the apple has a pleasing rotational symmetry when cut crosswise as well as the symmetry of the two sides when cut lengthwise. Giving children opportunities and time to draw encourages careful examination.

WHAT WE DO AND SAY

What can we see now?

I wonder what we might see?

I can see the same pattern going round and round.

What can we say about these shapes?

Oh! This one is different, look … Can you find another one like this?

BROADENING THIS OUT

- Take a 'branch' of leaves and look at it carefully. Ferns are interesting as they reproduce their pattern. The pattern in a fern is a *fractal*, which is a complex pattern that repeats at different scales. The fronds of a fern are a natural example of a fractal, with smaller fronds repeating the same shape along each stem: https://nrich.maths. org/fractals-0
- Explore sorting a selection of leaves into two different types, e.g. all the leaves which are pointy and the leaves that are not.
- Print with leaves. Can we match the leaf to the print? How do we know it is that leaf?

TASK: TRAIN TRACK OR ROAD MAT

PROVIDE

Train and/or road resources, including cars and playpeople. Add construction blocks to make bridges, etc.

Large rolls or sheets of paper and pens.

Figure 2.11   Road play

Figure 2.12   Indoor maps

THE MATHS

This task mainly develops children's *spatial* awareness and associated directional and positional language. There is a development through doing and talking about where they are in relation to other objects, to linking this to a representation, which is what small world play provides; it is a representation of the larger, outside world. This activity is about children experiencing representations and beginning to interact with them.

WHAT WE DO AND SAY

Let's make the longest track and put some houses along both sides.

What town shall we build today?

I wonder, can we make the track go under the bridge?

The road is straight. Can we turn a corner next?

I am driving this lorry along here and turning left here ...

BROADENING THIS OUT

- Invite children to use the large sheets of paper to plan a road or rail route. It can be displayed near the area for discussion.
- Model walking a playperson along the edge of the road (or driving a car) and narrating their route: "*Along the straight road, turn left here, over the crossing, under the bridge...*"
- Add journey story books to the area, e.g. *A Lion in the Night*, by Pamela Allen, or *Lucy in the City*, by Julie Dillemuth (see Section 3, p. 41).
- Add some real street maps of the local area to the play space.

TASK: DO A JIGSAW – EVERY DAY!

PROVIDE

A greeting card, a photocopy of a familiar book cover, or the front of a familiar cereal box, along with an identical one which is cut into two or three straight-sided or irregular pieces for children to fit together. You may wish to start by matching the pieces onto the whole picture and/or drawing an outline on a page as a 'frame' into which to fit the pieces.

THE MATHS

Jigsaws help children to understand how shapes fit together, how different shapes are constructed and the relationships between shapes. Research with 2-year-olds points to the importance of an adult sensitively supporting jigsaw play by chatting about the different shapes and properties like *straight, corner* and *fit,* and using directional words, like *turn* and *flip*, alongside appropriate gestures, to support this development (Levine et al. 2018). With experience, and as they develop, children use visualisation to predict what will fit and how, rather than using trial and adjustment.

WHAT WE DO AND SAY

Do you know this picture? What can you see? Can you point to a ...?

Let's see if we can make this whole again. I think I'll start with this piece....

(Continued)

What if we turn this piece around to see if it fits?

That piece fits exactly!

Do you think you can do this again if we muddle it back up?

BROADENING THIS OUT

- Hide one piece of the jigsaw to see if they notice one is missing.
- Cutting into more pieces (make sure you try it – it gets hard quite quickly!).
- Check you have a suitable range of (complete!) jigsaws to explore, from inset puzzles, through tray jigsaws with drawn outlines, to 4- to 12-piece jigsaws.
- Collect some different jigsaws and start a 'jigsaw club' with families or older children playing alongside the younger children.
- Cutting a square piece of plain card into four triangles by folding corner to corner (i.e. 'sandwich' shapes). Explore fitting them back together to make shapes and images. Encourage the children to name them – a house, a hat, a fish, etc.

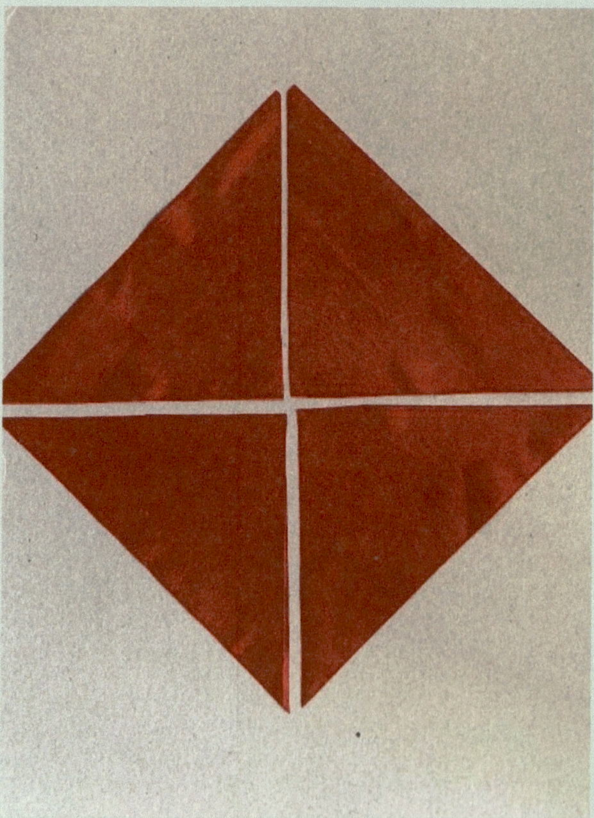

Figure 2.13   Four triangles

TASK: BLOCK PLAY

PROVIDE

A range of blocks and enough flat space to build with them. Play alongside children while they build their own structures, which may include them making long lines of identical shapes or towers. Build your own structures and narrate a commentary, or build collaboratively.

THE MATHS

As well as being important for children's physical development, block play is an essential element of *spatial learning*, leading to rich discussions about the properties of three-dimensional shapes (those that roll, stack, fit together, etc.), the shapes of the faces, the length of the edges and which match and fit, and making decisions about which shapes to choose for what they want to make.

Figure 2.14   Block play

Figure 2.15   Stacked unit blocks

(Continued)

The ideal collection of blocks are 'unit blocks', related to one other in shape and size, so that two shorter blocks match the length of one longer one, or two triangular prisms can be fitted together to make a cuboid, for example.

Providing time for children to play with these blocks leads to them repeatedly exploring the connections between these different shapes and different sizes, and how shapes are constructed and only then can they begin to predict and reason what shapes to use for different purposes.

Block play also involves creativity and visualisation, which are important elements of mathematical thinking. It is as important for older children as for younger ones.

WHAT WE DO AND SAY

Oooo, what shall we build today, I wonder?

I can see you have chosen the longer one to fit over that gap.

Shall we look for a shorter one to match that one?

Shall I take a picture of it when you have finished, so you can talk to us about it?

I wonder what you can add if you keep going?

Can you point to any blocks that are the same?

BROADENING IT OUT

Figure 2.16 Blocks outlined

- All children need extended time with the blocks to expand their ideas of what is possible. You will notice a development from lines and towers to the beginnings of enclosures and more complex constructions. Playing alongside children is an important way to support development, as is valuing their work by taking photographs and discussing the resulting creations.

- Keep a book of images of the children's constructions. Have them narrate about these for you to write alongside. Make this book available along with the blocks.
- Tidying away is another worthwhile spatial puzzle to solve. Mark the storage shelves with the outlines of the blocks for the children to match into position.
- Provide images of buildings to inspire creations.

INDOOR TASKS FOR OLDER, MORE EXPERIENCED CHILDREN

TASK: BOXES – MAKE SOMETHING

Figure 2.17 Making something

PROVIDE

A wide range of cardboard boxes and tubes, cereal boxes, small sheets of coloured card and/or magazine pages, scissors, tapes in dispensers (often quicker and easier to use than glue; if no dispensers are available, masking tape is easier to tear) and, if appropriate, staplers. Sit with the boxes and choose two to tape together, narrating what you are doing: *"I am going to stick this one on here to make it taller – it looks a bit like a rocket now…"*.

(Continued)

You can also consider providing some images of vehicles, buildings, machinery, etc. to stimulate ideas.

THE MATHS

While handling, exploring, combining and taking apart different-shaped boxes, children gain experience of the properties of various shapes and how they fit together (or not) and how similar and how different they are: *"Does this one stand up? Does this one roll? These are similar shapes but different sizes"*, etc. Narrating your decisions as you turn a box into something draws attention to the decisions you make about what to use and why.

Useful vocabulary to use may include: *flat, curved, sides, faces, edges, corners, point, sharp, sloping, cuboid, cylinder, prism, wedge, roof-shaped, arch, larger than, taller than, shorter than.*

WHAT WE DO AND SAY

Chatting about what we notice about the different shaped boxes, and accompanying this talk with gestures helps the children to understand the vocabulary we are using.

This tube is round. This box has a square face and it will fit on here, I think. Here is a much taller one.

This one has flat sides as well, but is smaller than yours.

I think this will stand up if I turn it up the other way.

What might you make (today)?

I see you have started with a big box/a tall tube. Let's see what's next.

Shall we take this box apart and see what shapes we can see?

Do you have a plan?

Can we find a box that would be a good shape for an arm, ... a roof, etc.

BROADENING THIS OUT

- Provide regular opportunities to construct in this way, which will develop children's imagination and creativity.
- Undo boxes to look at how they are made up of separate shapes (nets): "We could cut carefully down all these edges and open it up and see what it looks like? I think it might make a star shape, what do you think?"

TASK: FOLDING AND CUTTING

Figure 2.18   Folding and cutting

PROVIDE

A range of paper squares and rectangles in different sizes and (decent) scissors for children to explore folding and cutting. Children can be helped to make a firm fold by pressing along the fold and then cutting along the fold: *"What shapes have you made now you have cut along the fold?"* Model folding and cutting to change the shape of the paper you choose, narrating your decisions.

You may choose to provide larger sheets of paper for children to arrange the shapes they make.

THE MATHS

Deconstructing and constructing shapes is an important part of learning about fit, size and how different two-dimensional shapes are composed. We can support this development by introducing the vocabulary to describe what we see and what changes and what stays the same as we cut and fold.

WHAT WE DO AND SAY

Ooo I've cut two long thin rectangles – they could be legs!

I've folded this corner over – it looks a bit like a roof or a hat.

What is the same about these two? What is different about them?

(Continued)

What do you think you might see when you open your paper out?

I wonder if we can see any shapes that are the same …? Can you point to one the same as this one?

BROADENING THIS OUT

- You can provide a wider range of paper shapes – strips and variously sized offcuts.
- Children may like to arrange the shapes they make, collaboratively, into a design or a picture.
- Demonstrate how to make a hole in a piece of paper by folding and cutting on the fold – this activity can lead to all sorts of creativity!
- Roll sheets of A4 paper and tape them to create a family of cylinders (or a family of cones) of different sizes, heights and thicknesses.

Figure 2.19   Rolled cylinders

TASK: DRAW YOUR MODEL

Figure 2.20   Drawing a construction

PROVIDE

Clipboards (thick card and pegs) and a selection of pens and pencils together with the box of Duplo or Lego. *"Can we draw your model, so we know how to make it tomorrow?"* Collect the children's graphics to become a catalogue of their ideas.

Photographs of previously made models will stimulate both the construction and the graphics; or display Duplo models for ideas.

THE MATHS

Construction play is a rich stimulus for mathematical thinking for young children. Often it is difficult to see the mathematical relevance of such play, but imagining what we would like to make and bringing it to fruition by finding all the correct constituent parts uses our visualisation skills, and develops an ability to mentally take something apart and put it together again. (This is something we do with numbers when we calculate later. For example, If something costs 99p, I can pay with a £2 coin and know I will get £1 and 1p back as change).

Both interpreting and creating two-dimensional representations of something physical (i.e. something that is three-dimensional) are important aspects of spatial awareness.

(Continued)

It involves looking at objects in different ways, recognising similarities and differences and realising when something is the same object looked at from different points of view.

This task is for children who are experienced in playing with Duplo. To begin with, children may prefer to start building and only vocalise a name for their model after it is complete, or as their model develops. We can encourage them to plan ahead by saying things like "What are you thinking you might make today? What bricks can we use to make that?"

WHAT WE DO AND SAY

I like this model. I think I can make one the same if I start with these bricks.

Here's your clipboard for drawing how you make your model today.

Can you point to where in your drawing this brick is?

If I put your model here, so I can see it, I can draw it.

Do you think you have managed to draw every block you used?

Do you think we can have a go at making this model? What shall we start with?

BROADENING THIS OUT

- You may have access to Lego construction plans from sets that can be displayed and discussed.
- The children may become interested in drawing what they plan to make before they begin.
- Introduce drawing materials and clipboards into the block-play area, or outdoors with the large loose-parts play.
- Look at some architect's drawings together.

TASK: MY PATTERNS

PROVIDE

A selection of small loose parts, such as buttons, beads, nuts and bolts, along with paper plates, felt mats or small trays on which to arrange these items. Begin by making your own patterns alongside the children and narrating what you are doing. For example, *"I am choosing all these buttons because they are similar and I am going to put one at the middle of every side. Now I'm ....".*

Figure 2.21   My pattern

THE MATHS

A pattern is a predictable and regular relationship or sequence, usually involving numerical, spatial, or logical relations. Providing materials for pattern-making with loose parts will prompt children's spatial thinking as they choose and place their objects, i.e. which objects are placed in relation to each other and where on the plate or mat. They may choose to place something in each corner, or end-to-end around the edge. Often you will notice symmetrical choices. Moreover, identifying what is similar and what is different about objects is fundamental to thinking mathematically and children are using a same/different categorisation and identifying shape properties in selecting two or more of something to create a spatial pattern. For example, when finding and selecting four similar round objects to sit in each corner of a mat. For more information on the importance of pattern-making to mathematics, see Chapter Three, 'Mainly Number and Pattern', and The Education Hub website at: https://theeducationhub.org.nz/the-role-of-pattern-in-childrens-early-mathematical-understanding/

WHAT WE DO AND SAY

Can you tell me about your pattern?

(Offering an object – maybe one that doesn't seem to belong) Hmmm, *I wonder if this goes here …*

(Continued)

If you stand up and look at it, are you happy with your pattern?

Can you explain to me how to make one the same as yours?

Can you find a button that would fit here?

BROADENING THIS OUT

- Gradually you can model, and chat about, a rule you are using to select from a collection, such as all the shiny, round buttons, or all the longer bolts.
- You can very deliberately put an obviously 'wrong' item into your pattern and see if they spot the mistake.
- Take photos of the patterns and display them nearby for inspiration: can children identify how the pattern is made?
- Introduce mirrors for them to play with, standing these on the patterns they make.
- Focus on making repeating patterns on long strips of card. Research, particularly into repeating patterns, has found that children's patterning skills is predictive of their later mathematical competence (Mulligan et al. 2020). For more on this topic, see Chapter Three, 'Mainly *Number and Pattern*'.
- Take the task outside and explore pattern-making with natural, found items.
- Tape two plastic mirrors together and stand them up to make a hinged mirror-space for children to explore placing items inside.
- Explore standing and sliding single mirrors across postcards or other images.

Figure 2.22   Inside two mirrors

SECTION 3 – PICTURE BOOKS

The Early Childhood Mathematics Group has a comprehensive collection of story books that are useful for shape and space, as well as YouTube links, on their website: https://earlymaths.org/spatial-books/

Here are a few favourites:

A Lion in the Night, by Pamela Allen. A chase involving directions and a map.

Which One Doesn't Belong? Playing with shapes, by Christopher Danielson. Each page presents four shapes for children to decide for themselves which is the odd one out. There are no 'right answers' as there are different, equally correct ways of choosing.

Lucy in the City, by Julie Dillemuth. A young raccoon becomes separated from her family one night and has to find her way home.

Tangram Cat, by Maranke Rinck and Martijn van der Linden. This is an interactive book about a child who creates an imaginary cat from the seven Tangram pieces provided in the book. All the animals in the book can be made with the Tangram puzzle.

Marion Walter's Mirror books. These are out of print but available on some second-hand sites. They are interactive as they each contain a mirror and suggestions on a problem to solve involving the mirror and the book images.

RHYMES AND SONGS

Many nursery rhymes and songs use the vocabulary of movement and direction, such as Incy Wincy Spider going *up* and *down* the water spout, and 'We're going on a bear hunt', going *over, through,* etc. They are particularly effective when used with gestures and actions.

'Do as I'm doing' includes actions and you can perform any action for your children to follow. For example, rolling hands, jumping up and down, turning around, etc.

Do as I'm doing;

Follow, follow me!

Do as I'm doing;

Follow, follow me!

If I do it high or low,

If I do it fast or slow,

Do as I'm doing;

Follow, follow me!

Do as I'm doing;

Follow, follow me!

Figure 3.0   Collecting leaves and sticks

3

MAINLY NUMBER AND PATTERN

A 4-year-old counts backwards successfully from 20.

Adult: Did you learn that at Nursery?

Child: No, from the microwave.

SECTION 1 – ABOUT THIS AREA OF MATHS

If you ask people what mathematics means to them, many of the replies will be related to number: for example, fractions, algebra, equations, arithmetic, times (multiplication) tables, etc. These are often the more abstract areas of number, as well as those that may provoke negative memories for the person answering the question! This chapter is about supporting and empowering our, and our families', confidence to talk about the numbers around us with young children. Its aim is to realise the potential of everyday activities and routines for number-spotting games and discussions.

Learning within the mathematical area of 'number' consists of building understanding of the *composition* (properties) of number, including fractional numbers and large numbers, *comparing* these numbers and knowing how numbers relate to each other, and becoming fluent *operating* with these numbers. Seeking and exploring patterns is at the heart of mathematics (Schoenfeld 1992) because an awareness of pattern helps us to notice and understand mathematical relationships, for example, observing how the 10s-digit changes as each decade is counted in our number system: **13, 23, 33, 43, 53**…

We can organise early number understanding into the following areas, which are all interrelated:

- **Comparison** – involves knowing which numbers are *worth more* or *less* than one another, and how much larger or smaller (how many *more* or *fewer)* one number, or amount, is compared to another. Learning about comparison involves understanding *equality* and *inequality*.

- **Composition** – how one number or amount can be composed of (*made up from*) two or more smaller numbers or amounts, e.g. 5 being *composed* of 4 and 1, or 3 and 2.
- **Cardinality** – the *cardinal value* of a number refers to the quantity, or 'how-many-ness' of items the number represents. The last number you say when you count tells you how many are in the group all together. Cardinality understanding includes *subitising;* the instant recognition of a small amount without having to count each item, ie recognising and saying "Two!" or "Three!" without counting "one, two, three", etc.
- **Counting** – children enjoy learning and repeating the sequence of counting numbers long before they understand the cardinal values of the numbers or how each counting number is related to the following or previous one. Counting is a key way of establishing *how many* items there are, as the last number you say tells you how many are in the group. But first children need to enjoy saying the counting words in the correct order in many different contexts. Learning the counting system is linked to *pattern*, as after 9, the pattern of the digits is visible: 11, 12, 13, 14 … 21, 22, 23, 24 … Playing games involving number tracks, such as Snakes and Ladders or Ludo, are useful and are often enjoyable counting experiences for young children. *Number tracks,* where each square or space is numbered, are more appropriate at this age than *number lines,* where each division is numbered.

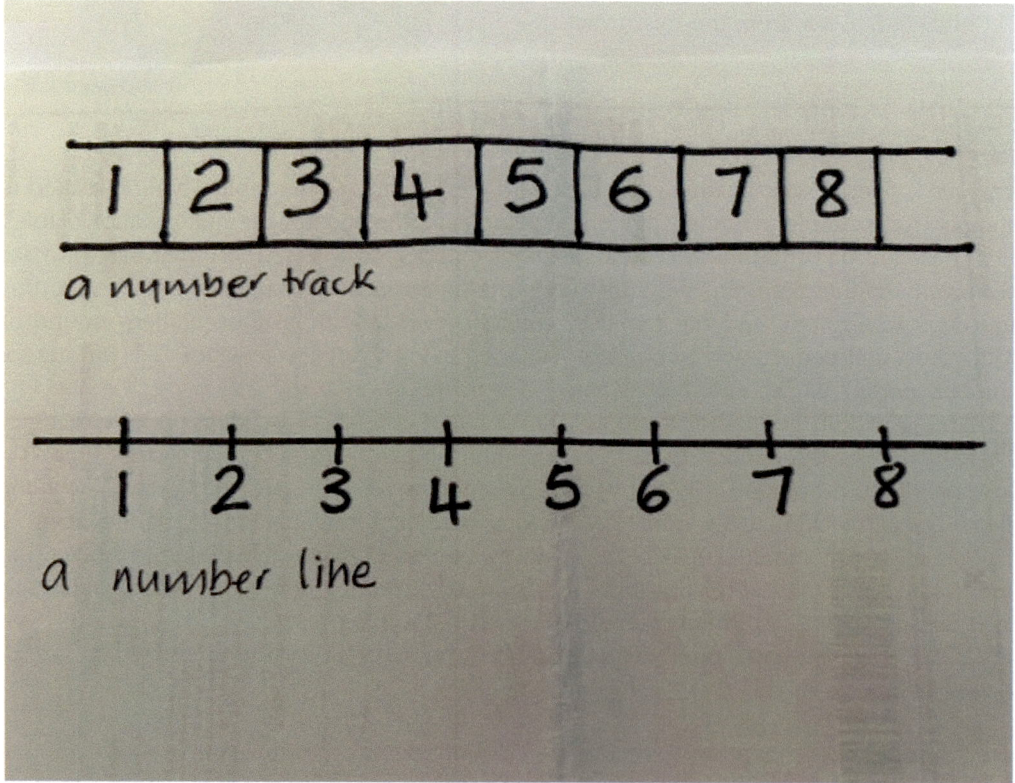

Figure 3.1   Number track, number line

- **Pattern** – virtually all mathematics is based on pattern. The patterns in our number system are central to number understanding, and it is worth noting that this is tricky! While the repeating pattern of the digits can be *seen* when numbers after 10 are written (e.g. 11, 12, 13, 14 … and 21, 22, 23, 24 …), it is not *heard* when we say these numbers in English, i.e. 'eleven' instead of onety-one, 'thirteen' instead of onety-three, etc. We can hear our youngest children trying to make sense of the system when they count like this: *"eighteen, nineteen, twenteen, thirtween …"* or *"twenty-eight, twenty-nine, twenty-ten …"*, for example.
- While the sequence of numbers is one key pattern, wider experiences of pattern-making are also important. Children can spot patterns in a range of contexts, such as printed patterns, which are often *symmetrical*, and in stories, which are often *repetitive* or involve an *increase*. An example of the latter is *Mr Gumpy's Outing*, by John Burningham. Research indicates that experience of *repeating* patterns and being able to identify the *unit that repeats* is key in predicting future mathematical development (Gripton 2022; Papic and Mulligan 2007), as pattern learning provides the foundations for later algebraic learning. Children often enjoy creating their own patterns with all sorts of objects, such as buttons, pinecones, leaves or blocks, as well as with movements and sounds, linking with music and rhymes.
- **Statistical reasoning** – as adults, we are surrounded by data and having to make sense of graphs, charts and figures. The beginnings of this sense-making are to talk about the likelihood of an event, to make comparisons between amounts and to encourage our children to think about what they notice.

The tasks in this chapter touch on all these aspects of number. It is the number aspect of mathematics that often generates the most heat! These tasks are focused on recognising children as active, numerical thinkers, who flourish on being nurtured rather than over-corrected. Children are rarely wrong in their answers; rather, they may have heard a different question from the one you are asking. Here is an example:

Child (4 years old):   What does 5 and 5 make?

Adult: 10 – see? [Holding up two hands] 5 and 5, that's 10 fingers altogether.

Child: No, NO! One and nought make 10, so what do 5 and 5 make?

What matters most when working numerically with children is that we are non-judgmental. We need to try to find out what the child is thinking. The best way to do so is to follow an answer by asking "Ooo, that's interesting, I wonder why you said that?" or expressing interest in hearing more. It is also important to ask "Are you sure?", even when a child answers correctly, rather than pouncing excitedly on a correct answer. Children need to become sure themselves, rather than rely on our praise to know if they are correct or not.

WHY IT IS IMPORTANT

Most of us recognise the importance of the area of mathematics known as 'number' in our lives. What is often less well recognised is the breadth and depth of understanding necessary for us to function confidently numerically. Number is broader than arithmetic and being *numerate* requires us not only to recall key number facts but also to flexibly apply these in many situations and draw on a range of strategies to solve a wide range of numerical problems.

Research has found that young children's mathematics understanding at the start of school predicts their future success, over and above even their reading and attention (Duncan et al. 2007). Young children who start school with a strong base in early number, based on a wide range of experiences, are at an advantage (Cahoon et al. 2021).

Figure 3.2   Bus numbers

Young children are interested in number symbols as they see and interact with them in many different contexts every day; for example, when they catch a bus, buy new shoes and think about how many sleeps it is until an anticipated event. In research with 3- to 5-year-olds, Voutsina and Stott (2023) found that there was great variation in children's experience of numerals, including numbers on thermostats, doses on medicine labels, a 24-hour clock display, selecting a TV episode, aisle numbers in a shop, pin numbers and speed signs. All these experiences provide rich discussion opportunities for young children and their families.

It is important that we recognise and build on children's curiosity by providing rich, playful experiences, with which they can build connections between these contexts. We can point out number symbols when they are used to show order (e.g. house numbers), measures (e.g. speed signs), quantity (e.g. food labelling) and as identifiers (bus numbers, shoe sizes). Because we use numbers in many ways, as well as for establishing quantity, making a clear connection between *numbers* and *quantities (cardinality)* can take three to four years in primary school (Nunes and Bryant, 2009), for example, recognising that 6 on a box of eggs relates to a quantity of 6 items. This connection is key to developing a deep and flexible understanding of numbers. Many of the numerals that children meet are unrelated to quantity but are used as identifiers. For example, we don't have another 10 shoes somewhere if we are size 11 and we don't have to count and wait for the first 23 buses if we want to catch bus number 24! Recognising, pointing out and talking about numbers in different contexts is important.

Figure 3.3 Subitising cards with numerals

FURTHER READING

Clements, D., & Sarama, J. (2021). Learning and teaching early math: The learning trajectories approach (3rd ed.). London: Routledge.

Gifford, S. (2018). Subitising. *nrich*, 23 October. https://nrich.maths.org/articles/subitising

Nunes, T., & Bryant, P. (2009). Key understandings in mathematics learning: Introduction and summary of findings. London: Nuffield Foundation.

Thouless, H., Gifford, S., Moses, K., & James, R. (2020). Reasoning about patterns. *Mathematics Teaching, 271*, 30–34.

Many 3-, 4-, and 5-year-olds enjoy the BBC TV series 'Numberblocks', where each of the numbers from 0–10 are given a personality and relationships with other numbers are explored. When watched with children, these programmes can promote rich number discussions.

SECTION 2 – TASKS

The following tasks explore number and pattern.

OUTDOOR TASKS FOR YOUNGER CHILDREN

TASK: PUDDLE JUMPING

Figure 3.4 Puddles

PROVIDE

While out for a wet walk, count the puddles to jump over or splash in. You may wish to count two or three jumps in each puddle, or you can jump once in the first puddle, twice in the second puddle, etc.

THE MATHS

This task is mainly about becoming familiar with the counting sequence (*counting*), beginning to link numbers to a small amount (*cardinality*) and enjoying ourselves as we count.

(Continued)

If you are counting the puddles, there will be different gaps in time between one puddle and the next and children will have to remember what number they have already said and then say the next one, which is a skill that leads later to *counting on* from one number to the next without starting from the beginning (1) again. Counting the number of jumps involves counting something that cannot be seen, and if you specify a number of jumps to count, the child has to remember to stop jumping at the correct amount – which they may find hard!

WHAT WE DO AND SAY

> You counted 1, 2, 3!
>
> I think we said 4 at the last puddle, so this one is puddle number 5.
>
> Shall we jump 3 times in this one?
>
> Let's remember that we counted 4 at that puddle.
>
> So, how many puddles is that so far... / altogether?
>
> Let's hold up 4 fingers, the same number as the puddles / jumps.

BROADENING THIS OUT

- Find a stick and tap a number of times to count, or drop stones into a pool to count.
- Find lots of opportunities to count – footsteps, buses, dogs on leads ... – and hold up the corresponding number of fingers.

TASK: A COUNTING LIST

PROVIDE

While out and about, find and then display: 1 pebble, 2 leaves, 3 short sticks .... Collaboratively, make your own counting list with the children. You may like to introduce numerals written on cards for children to match to each amount.

THE MATHS

This is a *cardinal* number activity, where we relate the spoken – and written – number to an amount. The connection between a numeral and its cardinal quantity is key to developing young children's nudber understanding. Many of the numerals that children meet are unrelated to quantity, but instead are used as labels. This task is an opportunity

Figure 3.5 Counting found items

to link a quantity with its numeral, as well as to put the numerals in order from *least* to *most*. It is also an opportunity for some *subitising* practice. *Subitising* is the instant recognition of a small amount without having to count each one – saying "Two!" or "Three!" without counting each one: "one, two, three", etc. Read more about subitising at: https://nrich.maths.org/articles/subitising

You may feel that it is appropriate to *compare* the amounts of each and to talk about whether there are *more* or *fewer* pebbles than sticks, for example, or to point out that there is *one more* each time. Laying out the pebbles clearly so that we can see each number is *one more* or *one fewer* than another is a physical example of a simple graph (*statistical reasoning*).

Figure 3.6 Pebble graph

(Continued)

WHAT WE DO AND SAY

I wonder ... how far we will count?

Let's fetch zero stones!

How do you know you have four sticks? Are you sure?

How many can you see? Show me on your fingers.

Wow! I see you're counting them ALL!

Let's line them up in order from the least to the most.

BROADENING THIS OUT

- Once 0–3 are displayed with their quantities, play a game. One item is secretly removed and children need to work out which numeral doesn't have the right amount of items.
- Muddle up the 0–3 numeral cards for children to sort out and then match to the correct amounts.
- Some children may like to make their own numeral labels for their own scavenged collections of small things. It is important that you support their own ways of recording, which may include attempts to write numerals (which may not be written 'correctly'), or forms of tally, as well as completely idiosyncratic mark-making. All of this is fine at this stage of development, as what is important is that they are attaching a written mark to signify an amount.

Figure 3.7   My own recording

TASK: LINE OF STICKS

Figure 3.8   Line of sticks

PROVIDE

Opportunities to collect a range of sticks and a space to lay them out in a long line. Start by laying a few sticks end to end, counting them together as you go. Invite children to make the line longer by adding more sticks and counting them along with you. How high can we count? How long will the line be if we count to 20?

THE MATHS

Engaging in this task provides opportunities to *count* collaboratively as high as you wish, and to *tag* (touch) each stick as you say the counting word. There is a lot to remember and to co-ordinate when counting, and young children often get their tagging out of sync with their spoken counting sequence. We can support them by exaggerating the tagging and reminding them to touch each stick as we say the next count word.

Finally, you can draw their attention to the *cardinal* amount (the number of sticks altogether in the line) by indicating the whole line and repeating the final number said. Many children will enjoy counting higher and higher. It is important that we don't restrict them, but instead encourage their interest in the later parts of the count sequence, as it becomes more regular after the teens. This task links to *measures* and experiencing how the size of a unit affects a length; i.e. you need fewer long sticks to stretch further.

(Continued)

WHAT WE DO AND SAY

You add yours now, that will be 8, 9, 10!

That is a lot of short sticks – how many do you think you have collected? If we count 30 sticks, do you think the stick line will reach that fence?

Wow! You have found a lot of sticks, let's make a long line and count them together.

And one more stick makes ....?

BROADENING THIS OUT

- Lay out up to 5 or 6 sticks in a line and then count backwards as you remove them one at a time to "zero sticks!"
- Explore:
  - choosing only longer sticks, which will take fewer to make a long line
  - how far lots of little sticks reach.
- Make shapes and patterns using sticks. For example, "I wonder if we can make a circle big enough for us all to stand inside?"
- Make a tall tower of sticks by laying them across one another, or building them into a teepee shape *(measures – height)*.

OUTDOOR TASKS FOR OLDER, MORE EXPERIENCED CHILDREN

TASK: NATURAL PATTERNS

Figure 3.9   Organising into rows

PROVIDE

Children collect natural items with which to make patterns. To begin, invite children to 'make a pattern', which you can narrate: "*I see you have chosen to put one leaf in every corner of that paper*". Gradually, they may begin to describe what they create. Next, provide long strips of card with double-sided tape attached to lead to making *repeating* patterns, that go on and on, over and over again, from the beginning to the end of the strip.

THE MATHS

Research, particularly into repeating patterns, has found that children's patterning skills are predictive of their later mathematical competence (Mulligan and Mitchelmore 2009). The research highlights children's ability to recognise that the part of the pattern that repeats (the *unit of repeat*) is what is important in terms of mathematical development. Gradually, you can draw their attention to how a long pattern repeats over and over, where it begins each time and how easy it is to *predict* what comes *next* in the pattern. It may be a simple ABAB pattern, where two different items alternate, or a more complex ABBA, ABBA or AABC, AABC patterns, where different numbers of items appear in each repeat. You may feel that it is appropriate to talk about *how many* of each item you have used, *subitising* the small amounts: "*1 stick, 2 leaves, then 1 stick again, 2 leaves, … what's next I wonder?*".

(Continued)

WHAT WE DO AND SAY

I really want to know more about your pattern, I can see …

I'm going to use these three different shells to make a pattern that repeats, over and over.

What can you see in my pattern? Can you point to the leaf that is the same as this one?

Let's try to make a pattern that reaches right around the edge of this plate.

Look at Bryah's pattern, how does it go?

BROADENING THIS OUT

- Provide a range of found items for pattern-making that don't simply rely on colour.
- Collect and chat about patterns on materials and wallpapers, for example.
- Provide photographs of patterns that have been made and invite children to make one *the same as* or *different from* ….
- Tap a stick to make a short numerical/musical pattern for children to listen to and to copy.
- Use your bodies to make repeating patterns, e.g. clap, clap, stamp, clap, clap …
- Try to draw your repeating pattern.

TASK: JUMPSCOTCH

PROVIDE

Together, draw a hopscotch grid into sand, earth or in chalk.

Figure 3.10   Hopscotch

Number the squares from 1 to 9. Enjoy jumping or hopping from square to square, in order, calling out the numbers as you land on them. Repeat backwards from 9 to 1. Eventually, you may feel that it is appropriate to introduce the traditional game of rolling a pebble onto each square in turn, missing this square out when you jump/hop to the top of the grid and back, calling out the numbers landed on each time.

THE MATHS

This is an oral *counting* activity, where children learn and practice *counting up and back* from 1 to 9, linking the counting word to each written *numeral*. Counting backwards is as important to learn as counting forwards and may become popular if you introduce "Zero!" or "Blast off!" as you land back off the grid.

When playing the traditional hopscotch game, children miss out numbers in turn, practising continuing a count with a missing (or whispered) number. They will have to remember which number they have already said and then say the one after the missing

(Continued)

one, which is a skill that leads later to *counting on* (or back) from one number to the next without starting from the beginning again.

WHAT WE DO AND SAY

Count with me as I jump.

I'll count as you land on the squares.

Now backwards ... 9, 8, 7 ...

The stone is on 3 – now we miss 3 out. Let's try from 1.

BROADENING THIS OUT

- Invite children to draw their own hopping or jumping tracks to play on, and to invent their own games.
- Extend the grid or line above 10 to practise teen-counting.
- Take this game indoors and use playpeople jumping on a paper grid numbered 1–9.

TASK: SOCK THROW

Figure 3.11   Sock throw

Figure 3.12   Counting socks

PROVIDE

Four small socks filled with some sand or lentils or something similar, and tied tightly at the top. A large hoop or tyre, laundry basket or other items can act as a target. Children take turns to throw the four sand-socks at the target. At each turn they say how many are in the target and how many are outside the target.

THE MATHS

This is a *composition* task, where children explore the different ways of *partitioning* a quantity: 4 in and none out, 2 in and 2 out, 1 in and 3 out, etc. Children also practise their *subitising* skills, as they recognise each small amount from 1 to 4 without having to count every sock each time.

By fixing the quantity of socks (the quantity of socks we play with is given and stays constant), children are *partitioning* a quantity, making it easier to calculate or visualise how many are 'hidden' when we can see the remainder: i.e. "*I can see 1 out so 3 must be in!*" This method helps children gradually to memorise these number facts. If we change the number of socks we throw every time, they have to *combine* two amounts, usually by counting.

(Continued)

As children become familiar with the game, you can introduce a large scoreboard and pen.

WHAT WE DO AND SAY

Two in and two out – that's four altogether.

Four in and ZERO out!

Shall we keep our scores each time?

How many are in, if you see three outside?

BROADENING THIS OUT

- Look at their scoreboards together later, to allow the children to talk about what happened.
- Change the quantity of socks to play with: three or five.
- Number the hoops or baskets and throw that many in.
- Hide four playpeople or four pieces of treasure in a tray of sand to dig up. How do children know how many are left to find?

TASK: WRITING MY NUMBERS

PROVIDE

Wet sand or a muddy surface, strong sticks. Children draw numerals in the sand/mud. Model writing 1, 2 and 3 yourself, and invite children to trace over these, starting at the top of each. They can 'write' them with a finger in the palm of their hands, while being able to see the mud-numbers.

Over time, you can develop this into a game, where you or a child *starts to* write a numeral and the others have to say which it is, or find the matching number from a set of cards, or hold up that number of fingers, find that number of items, clap or jump that number of times, and so on.

THE MATHS

This task is about recognising, reading and writing *number symbols*. Children will meet different ways to write numerals and need to eventually recognise them all.

Figure 3.13   A variety of numerals

(Continued)

If this task is developed as suggested, numerals are linked to their *quantity*, a connection which is key to developing number understanding.

WHAT WE DO AND SAY

Where have you seen this number?

Is this 'your' number, Luna? Why is that?

Let's try to write this ... really HUGE... very tiny.

How many jumps shall we do this time?

BROADENING THIS OUT

- Partially cover some drawn numerals and ask children to identify the number as you gradually expose it: "What can this be?"
- You (or the children) can make a set of 0–5 cards to play with or for labelling the bikes and their parking places.
- Link this task with 'A counting list' (see outdoor tasks for younger children on p. 50). Collect exactly 3 ... 6 ... found items. Draw a large number track and place the correct quantity of leaves on each number (a *number track* consists of squares which are numbered, as on a snakes and ladders board).
- On a dry or sunny day, write numerals with water and paintbrushes. Can we jump that many times before they dry?
- Lay out numeral cards and calculators for children to play with.

INDOOR TASKS FOR YOUNGER CHILDREN

TASK: COUNTING STAIRS AND STEPS

PROVIDE

Some steps or stairs to count. Walk up and down the steps regularly, counting as you land a foot on each step (rather than counting the motion of stepping).

Gradually, you can count forwards when you go up: 1, 2, 3, 4, 5, and backwards from the largest number, when you go down: 5, 4, 3, 2, 1. Counting backwards is as important as counting forwards and often needs more practice.

Figure 3.14   Counting tree steps

THE MATHS

This task is about learning the *counting words* and learning their *order*, and becoming fluent, both forwards and backwards. Counting steps and stairs is often an activity young children and their families enjoy doing together. Valuing and talking to families about how important counting is, as well as how to include backwards counting, in their home languages as well as in English, will support and empower family members to chat confidently about numbers at home.

WHAT WE DO AND SAY

One, two – that's it, say the number when we're on the step, three …

Six – we're at the top now! Great counting!

(Continued)

Let's go back down and count them again.

We're going down – let's count back to zero: six, five…

BROADENING THIS OUT

- Build a set of steps using blocks. Make a toy walk up and make a mistake counting the stairs. Do the children notice? Can they teach the toy what to say?
- Count along paving slabs or stepping stones.
- Bang a stick along a fence and count each panel as you tap it.

TASK: MY NUMBERS

Figure 3.15   My numbers

PROVIDE

Families can collect on a smartphone as a photo montage or bring in pictures of numbers they have chatted about at home, or numbers they have found in their house. Images may include birthday cards, door or bus numbers they are familiar with, the time they go to bed, numbers on food containers, etc.

THE MATHS

This task is about recognising *numerals* and *number symbols*. Numbers are used in all sorts of complex ways, e.g. to label and distinguish between similar items (buses, houses or shoe sizes), to mark time (06:00, 18:00, 6 o'clock) and to communicate sizes in different ways (height 83 cm, age 3–4, 500 g). This activity is an opportunity to encourage children – and families – to notice numbers and to read them in a variety of different situations and to chat about what they signify each time.

WHAT WE DO AND SAY

63 – here is our bus, look – there is the number. That's how we know which bus to catch.

You're three and there are three candles on that card.

Can you point to number 2? 100 … ?

Adio lives at number 41. Let's find it … it's a 4 and a 1.

BROADENING THIS OUT

- Display the collection of numbers at child-height for discussion. If you work in a pre-school setting, display the collection in an area where carers and families collect their children.
- Provide a collection of 0–9 wooden numerals or numerals written on cards for children to play with. They might like to attach numerals to the bikes "You're on bike number 3", and line them up.
- Draw a 0–50 (or 100!) number line and add your family's names next to their ages. Talk about big numbers and start a scrap book of numbers.
- Lay the table for a fruit snack: "One cup for you, one for me… one piece of apple for everyone".
- Line up the toys and give each toy … 2 pieces of treasure – let the child choose the amount each time.

TASK: UNDER THE CUPS

Figure 3.16   Under the cups

PROVIDE

Six identical cups or tubs and 12 small items of a similar size or shape, such as pebbles or pasta shapes. Together, hide 1, 2 or 3 pebbles under the cups so that there are two cups covering 1 item, two cups covering 2 items and two cups covering 3 items. Make sure the items you choose don't cover each other up when the cups are moved.

Children choose two cups to lift up to see if the amount hiding under each cup matches, i.e. whether they both hide 1 (or 2 or 3) items.

THE MATHS

This game of hiding and finding amounts from 1 to 3 is about recognising small quantities – *cardinality* – and identifying the quantities without needing to count each item individually (*subitising*). It also allows *comparing* one small amount with another, to see if they are *equal*, or whether there are *more* or *fewer*. Mathematically, it is not as important to remember which cup is hiding which amount, as it is to practise recognising the amounts and comparing them.

WHAT WE DO AND SAY

Let's hide these two pebbles under this cup and these two under this cup …

What do you see?

I am going to look under this cup … oooo, I can see one! I wonder which other cup is hiding only one…?

Is that the same amount? No? Let's find the same amount.

BROADENING THIS OUT

- Muddle the cups' positions after each turn.
- Introduce a cup hiding nothing!
- Change the amounts played with: eg two to four pebbles.
- As children become more experienced, you can use this idea to play a more structured game of 'Pairs', where you take it in turns to lift only two cups to find the matching amounts.
- Secretly hide a number of small toys, fir cones or similar objects in a cloth bag. Pass the bag around a group of children sitting in a circle, and on a signal (when the music stops?) the bag is tipped out to see how many objects are hiding inside. Remember that counting dissimilar objects is often more challenging than counting identical objects.
- Play 'count and move'. Shout out a number and the children have to clap or jump or stamp or tap their knees or sit down that number of times.

INDOOR TASKS FOR OLDER, MORE EXPERIENCED CHILDREN

TASK: HANDFULS

Figure 3.17   Take a handful

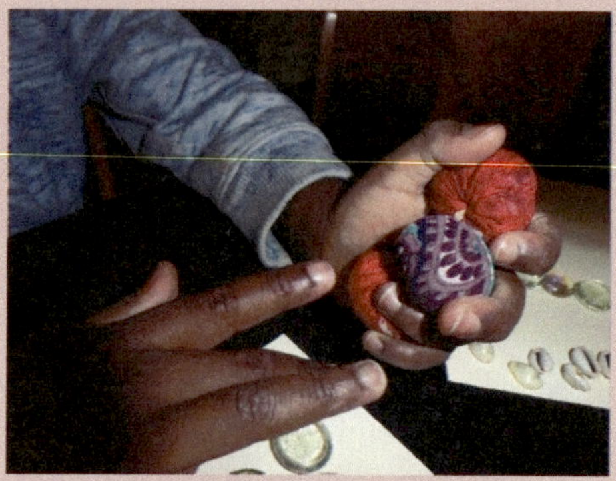

Figure 3.18   Handful

PROVIDE

A tray of smallish, similar-sized items in different colours, such as counters or buttons, or bolts and nuts, and paper plates or similar, enough for one for each child.

Children take a handful from the mixed tray and tip it onto their plate to organise to see what they grabbed, and to compare the differing amounts of items. Remember, the smaller the items, the more they will hold in their hands!

THE MATHS

This task is an opportunity to *organise*, *count* and *compare* amounts, and to experience *equality* and *inequality* as *more* or *fewer* (*fewer* is the correct word to use for discrete – individual and separate – items. *Less* is the term to use in continuous situations, where something continues without stopping, e.g. water or string).

Each handful will be different, so there is a lot to compare. To begin with, it will be enough to chat about the different items in their handful: *"Two red ones and three blue and …"*.

You can choose to restrict the tray selection to two colours and compare the quantity of each colour in their handful compared to their friend's – or your – handful.

There is also an element of *statistical analysis* embedded in this task, and the *probability* (likelihood) of the next handful being the same or different.

WHAT WE DO AND SAY

What might be in my/your handful this time, I wonder?

Oooo, more red ones, I think!

What did you grab this time? Let's see ...

Can you sort these out so we can easily see ...

Let's see if there are more/fewer nuts or more/fewer pebbles.

BROADENING THIS OUT

- This is a task that can be played repeatedly, with different collections, to suit you and your children. Some children simply enjoy grabbing a lot of items and will try to grab the most − more than anyone else. They may be less interested in looking at what their handful consists of. This is of course fine and will involve a lot of counting and comparing larger amounts!
- If you use cubes, it is easy to make towers to compare the *heights* of different quantities. If you use items of different sizes, it is often more challenging for children to compare amounts.
- Roll a dotty dice and "say it fast" by looking at the dots and covering the dice before saying how many dots there are.

Figure 3.19　Graph of coloured stones

TASK: TWO MIRRORS

Figure 3.20   Inside two mirrors

PROVIDE

A collection of small loose parts, such as buttons, beads, pebbles, shells, etc., or playpeople. Using unbreakable safety mirrors, hinge two together with tape so that they stand up.

Place one button at a time into the hinged space and focus on the number of buttons we can see each time, as well as what happens to the quantity when the mirrors are moved in and out. Changing the angle of the mirrors by moving them in and out will alter the number of buttons you see. Children can explore by placing chosen items in the space contained by the hinged mirrors to peer in and see what happens to the quantity. At first, they may put in as many as possible, giving you an opportunity to talk about large numbers: *"Do you think there are 100? 1000? ..."*.

THE MATHS

This task is an exciting *counting* and *cardinality* opportunity, as the quantity of items increases (and decreases) as the mirrors are moved and as we play with the idea of the different amounts we can make appear. *Rotational patterns (part of the area of mathematics known as shape and space)* are also part of the experience and beautiful kaleidoscopic patterns can be produced quite simply by choosing what to place in front of the mirrors and how to move the mirrors. The experience allows for exploration of *what happens when* you place an item or items inside the space, and *what happens if* you move the mirrors in and out. It is an opportunity for some *mathematical thinking* associated with creativity and prediction as well as *mathematical talk* when describing and explaining what they see.

WHAT WE DO AND SAY

What will you try now? How are you choosing to place those?

I can see six altogether. I wonder, can we make fewer? Can we make them disappear?

I am wondering what will happen if I put these three here ...

Let's try ...

Wow! I didn't expect to see that many! Did you?

BROADENING THIS OUT

- Change the items to use with the mirrors. Maybe use small blocks and playpeople. What would the children like to try?
- Explore running a single mirror over a simple picture, such as one from a picture book: *"Can we make more people? Can we make the people disappear?"*
- Read Marion Walter's Mirror books (you can read a review at: https://mathshistory. st-andrews.ac.uk/Extras/Walter_books/) and leave them out for the children to play with and explore.

TASK: HIDING A NUMBER

PROVIDE

Make a set of 0–6 numeral cards with the children. (You might prefer to begin with the numerals 0–4). When they are finished, place them in a line and in order from 0 on the left to 6 on the right. Take it in turns to turn one card over (to hide the numeral) and for children to say which one is hiding. As they become more confident, they can cover their eyes as one card is turned.

Figure 3.21   Making number cards

THE MATHS

This game is focused on *reading and recognising numerals* and learning the *order* of the counting numbers in a playful way. The order of numerals 0–9 must be seen regularly in many contexts to be learned and for children to become confident recognising them. Spotting numerals in the outside environment is important, especially as the fonts often differ.

This task can be linked to '*A counting list*' (see outdoor tasks for younger children on p. 50) to develop *cardinality*, by linking numerals to their quantities.

WHAT WE DO AND SAY

Can you point to 4? It's your age, isn't it!

Which number is hiding now? I wonder how you know?

Let's count along to find which number is missing, zero, one …

BROADENING THIS OUT

- Remove the chosen card to hide and close the gap in the row of cards.
- Can they recognise which numeral card is missing if they are not in order? You may like to begin this activity with just the numeral cards 0–3.
- Over time, extend the cards to 8, then 10, and begin the line at different starting points, e.g. 3–7.
- Explore a pack of playing cards together – what do we notice?

TASK: COPY THIS PATTERN

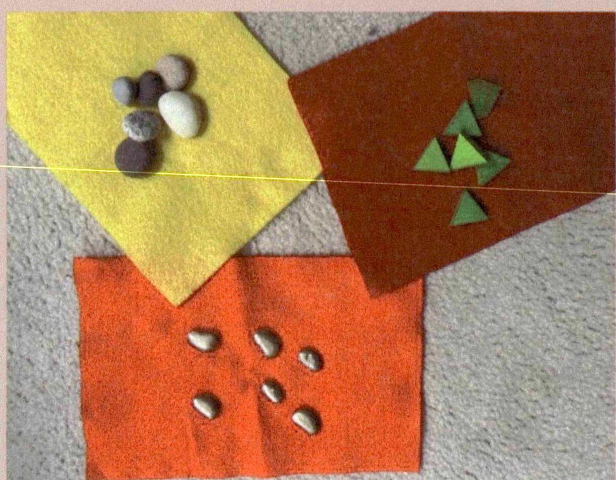

Figure 3.22   Six items

PROVIDE

For yourself and for each child: six similar items, such as pebbles, counters or corks; a 'mat', such as a sheet of card or a felt square; plain paper and black pens.

After children have explored arranging their six items freely on their mat, invite them to try to copy your pattern. Arrange your six items as a 1, 2, 3 triangle.

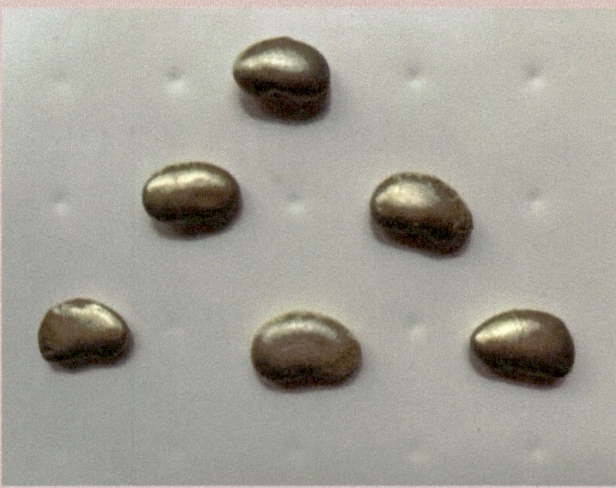

Figure 3.23   1, 2, 3 triangle

To begin with, the children may prefer to 'shadow' you and place their items one at a time as you do. It is helpful if the child sits alongside you to copy, as copying while viewing upside down or at an angle is more demanding.

THE MATHS

Noticing pattern (elements that are organised according to a *rule* or set of rules) is fundamental to mathematics, as *regularity* allows for *predictions* to be made about what goes where or what comes next. *"Virtually all mathematics is based on pattern and abstracting these patterns is the goal of mathematics learning"* (Gripton 2022: 3).

Three broad types of pattern are developmentally appropriate for children under five years of age to engage with: *spatial structure patterns* (arrangements), *repeating patterns* (repeated units) and *growing patterns* (which are based on a rule of increase – this is more challenging). Other tasks that are good starting points for noticing and discussing patterns include: '*Natural patterns*' (in this chapter, p. 54) and '*Leaf and fruit shapes*'(in Chapter Two, 'Mainly Shape and Space', on p. 26). The 'Six items' task invites children to examine how a *spatial structure* pattern is constructed. It includes an element of *growth* as each line increases by 1 each time. If they copy the whole pattern, you will be able to see how they are paying attention to the structure of the pattern, and to the quantity in each line.

WHAT WE DO AND SAY

> You choose where to place your five pebbles. Oh! One in each corner and one in the middle!

> I'm looking carefully at your pattern to see if I can make one exactly the same as yours – can you check for me?

> I wonder if that is exactly the same as mine?

BROADENING THIS OUT

- Invite the child to draw the 1, 2, 3 pattern.
- Try a different pattern to recreate, such as a grid of dots or/and an empty box shape.
- Two children might like to use familiar resources to take it in turns to be 'teacher' and 'copier', where one makes a pattern and teaches their partner how to make one just the same.

(Continued)

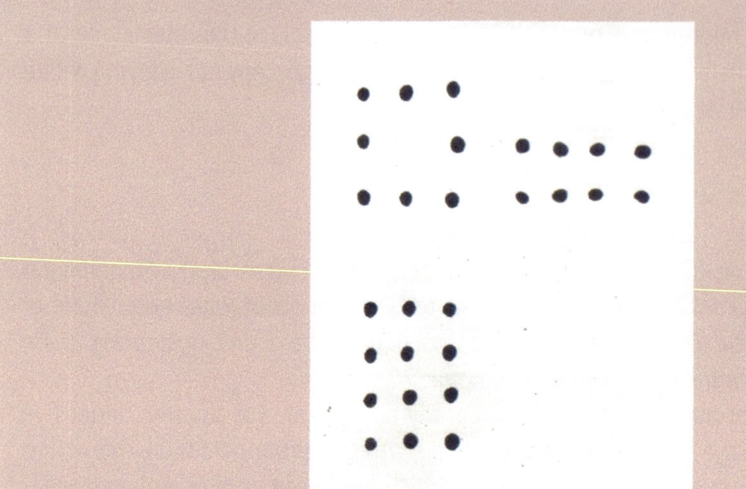

Figure 3.24   Dot arrangements

- Play 'Which One Doesn't Belong'. Provide four biscuits or playpeople or leaves and ask the children to point to the one they think *does not belong.* Can they say why? There are no right and wrong answers, as there may be a multitude of reasons for picking the odd-one-out (e.g. "I don't like that one", or "It's fatter", or "It's not red"). What is important is for the child to think about the *similarities* and *differences* between items and to try to explain a choice they make.

SECTION 3 – PICTURE BOOKS AND RHYMES

The Early Childhood Mathematics Group has a comprehensive collection of story books that are useful for number and pattern, as well as YouTube links, on their website: https://earlymaths.org/maths-picture-books/

Here are a few favourites:

Danielson, C. (2018). *How Many? A Counting Book.* Beautiful photographs of different things to count into the 20s. The child decides what to count on each page.

Gravett, E. (2016). *Bear and Hare: Where's Bear?* A hide-and-seek game where each time the searcher counts to 10. Many 1–10 counting books do not include written numerals, but this one does.

Fromental, J.-L., & Jolivet, J. (2017). *365 Penguins.* One penguin arrives each day of the year from 1 January. A fabulous exploration of one more and of big numbers.

Hesselberth, J. (2020). *Pitter pattern.* Repeating patterns using familiar objects to explore and discuss.

Pinczes, E., & MacKain, B. (1993). *One Hundred Hungry Ants.* 100 ants arrange themselves in different rectangular arrays to reach a picnic, e.g. two rows of 50, 10 rows of 10, etc.

Pulley Sayre, A., & Sayre, J. (2003). *One is a Snail, Ten is a Crab.* The numbers of feet are counted and combined to make numbers to 10, then in tens to 100. A lot to discuss.

National Geographic Kids Look and Learn Series: *Patterns!* Photographs of various repeating patterns to discuss and continue.

RHYMES AND SONGS

Five little squirrels sat up in a tree (Hold up five fingers)

The first squirrel said, "Well, what do I see?" (Point to fingers in turn)

The second squirrel said, "I see a dog!"

The third squirrel said, "I see a frog!"

The fourth squirrel said, "Let's run into the shade!"

The fifth squirrel said, "I'm not afraid!"

Then RUFF went the dog, and away the squirrels ran,

Five, four, three, two, one, NONE! (Fold fingers down one at a time)

(Hold up the number of fingers)

One little, two little, three little raindrops

Four little, five little, six little raindrops,

Seven little, eight little, nine little raindrops

Ten little raindrops, falling down.

Figure 4.0   A stick that is taller than me

4

MAINLY MEASURES

Sam (3 years 10 months) is holding his cutlery vertically, a knife, fork and a spoon, resting the handles on the table. He is referencing Teletubbies, a BBC children's programme.

Sam: This fork is Dipsy. 'Cos it's taller, and this one is Po [a spoon, the shortest] and this [the middle-sized knife] is La-La and Dipsy.

Adult: Who is taller out of Dipsy and La-La?

Sam: Dipsy's taller out of La-La and Po.

SECTION 1 – ABOUT THIS AREA OF MATHS

The mathematical area referred to as 'measures' encompasses the following topics, all to do with establishing a *quantitative* description of the *dimensions* or features of something:

- Length, circumference and height (linear measure).
- Area (two-dimensional measure).
- Weight (otherwise known as mass).
- Volume and capacity – *volume* is the total amount of space taken up by an object, *capacity* is the quantity contained by an object.
- Time – duration, or time passing, is measured in different units, such as month, hour, season, etc.

WHY IT IS IMPORTANT

Toddlers engage with measurement concepts as they play, when they react to the height of block towers being built, or struggle to move something heavy. As they get older, they can show an interest in measures they meet every day, such as when travelling in a car or bus (*"How far?"*, *"How long?"*), eating and cooking (*"We need more flour"*, *"Is it ready yet?"*) and getting to grips with when things take place (*"When is it my birthday?"*). They tend to use non-specific words such as 'big' and 'small' to refer to shape and size in length, weight and volume, or 'sleeps' in relation to time. They are often fascinated by the measuring tools adults use, such as tape-measures, scales, thermometers or timers, and valuable discussions can take place when children interact and play with these items (see Figures 4.1 and 4.2).

Figure 4.1   Tape measure and blocks

In our everyday lives we use *comparison* to answer questions such as *"How much longer is this?"* or *"Is this tall enough?"*. We do this by either *direct* comparison, by laying or standing objects next to one another, or *indirectly*, by using a measuring tool such as a tape measure. The latter is often more accurate but much more sophisticated, and we would not expect children under the age of 7 to be working with centimetres. Young children do need to meet and chat about the large range of *standard units of measurement* in use, such as centimetres, miles, kilograms, pints, etc.

Length, weight, volume and capacity are more visible and thus more accessible for younger children than measurements of time. Although time is complex (see below!), young children are interested in it, as it impacts their daily lives so much: *"Hurry up, we're going to be late"*, *"In a minute"*, *"It's bedtime, let's read a story"*, *"It's a long walk. It will take us an hour, so we'll need the buggy."*

Figure 4.2 4-year-old's tape measure recording

All children benefit from a rich variety of experiences to develop both their interest in, and understanding of, measures. What is important is that we support young children's interests, enrich their language and vocabulary, explore and discuss accuracy and the different *standard units* we use. Measures is a perfect context for embedding and applying children's developing number knowledge: *"We need five more bricks to make these towers the same height"*, or *"three cupfuls will fill this jug"*.

Standard measurement is more complex in the UK where we use a combination of *metric* and *imperial* units to measure. For example, a child will likely experience adults talking about distance in miles, length in metres (in a swimming pool, for example), height in feet and inches, and weights in stones, pounds and in grams. There is a lot of vocabulary to understand and use in the correct context and it will take years to embed. Whilst in primary school, children will be taught using the metric system (*kilograms, grams, litres, millilitres, metres, centimetres, millimetres,* etc.), but it will not harm children to talk about – and use – imperial units (*pounds, pints, miles, feet,* etc.). In the interaction that follows, an almost 4-year-old is beginning to use some measuring vocabulary with a varying degree of accuracy.

Figure 4.3   Alice's scales

Alice and mum are baking using pan scales. Mum puts the two weights on one side of the scales, one of 2 ounces and one of 1 ounce.

Adult: You want three ounces of sugar.

Alice looks at the two weights for a short while, picks up a spoon and counts 3 spoonfuls into the scale pan, counting.

Alice: One, two, three. [Pause] I have put quarter-to-three in and it's still not balancing.

WEIGHT AND LENGTH

Children need a lot of experience of carrying heavy items and hearing an adult say 'heavy' or maybe struggling with a bag and taking a few items out *"Ooph this is heavy… it's lighter now!"* etc. to begin to recognise what *light* and *heavy* mean. 'Light' is particularly tricky as children will be much more familiar with turning a light on or off! It is worth remembering that comparing the weights of different objects is more difficult that comparing their lengths. We can line up more than two objects to compare their lengths, but we can only compare the weights of two objects at a time, as we only have two hands, and balance (e.g. bucket) scales have only two pans. There are also different types of scale that children will see being used: digital scales, a pan with weights on one side, bathroom scales, and even hanging scales. In the early years, it is enough that they experience these items through playful activity and see us using and talking about them. *Contingent talk* in measures situations is central to developing young children's understanding. Put simply, this is when an adult notices what the child has become interested in and then starts to talk to them about it: *"You're picking up all the long sticks! I wonder if I can find a longer one"*.

TIME

There is far more to understanding time than learning to 'tell' the time. Understanding time is about being able to compare and measure duration (how long something lasts). Time is both continuous and intangible, making it difficult to measure; and we use many different units to measure it. We use discrete units, such as years, months, hours, minutes and seconds, and we make comparisons using a very wide range of vocabulary: *yesterday, next week, soon, in a minute, after, before, longer than, ages, weekend, etc*. We also use two different systems to tell the time: digital (such as on a microwave) and analogue (such as a traditional clock face). Time can also be 'told' using the 12- or 24-hour clock. Learning about time is a long process that takes children well into much later childhood.

In the early years, talk that refers to the order of events over time is important, alongside introducing new vocabulary and language in familiar contexts: *"Yesterday we did …, but today we are … "*, *"First we're going to go to the shop, next we'll take the car to the garage, then go to the library"*. More informal ways of measuring time, such as counting how many 'sleeps' until an event, or using a sand timer to mark shorter episodes, such as how long to clean our teeth, are also helpful. Some settings make 'count down' charts (like a calendar without dates) where the number of days to a big event can be crossed off. The routine of the day as a visual timetable is a valuable experience, providing plenty of opportunities to reinforce the sequence of the day and to use the language of time, such as *before, next, first, then,* etc.

You will find that some activities in this chapter are more suitable for your younger children and some tasks will better suit older children. There is a lot of mathematical development between the ages of 18 months and 4 years. It is important to dwell on – and wallow in – our favourite activities rather than 'pushing on'.

FURTHER READING

Although measurement is an important component of mathematics education, research on the learning and teaching of measurement is limited. The work of Julie Sarama and Doug Clements in the USA, which is accessible and free on their website, is most useful: www. learningtrajectories.org

Sarama, J., Clements, D. H., Barrett, J. E., Cullen, C. J., Hudyma, A., & Vanegas, Y. (2021). Length measurement in the early years: Teaching and learning with learning trajectories. *Mathematical Thinking and Learning, 24*(4), 267–290. https://doi.org/10.1080/10986065.2020.1858245

Szilagyi, J., Sarama, J., & Clements, D. (2013). Young children's understandings of length measurement: Evaluating a learning trajectory. *Journal for Research in Mathematics Education, 44*(3), 581–620. https://doi.org/10.5951/jresematheduc.44.3.0581

In relation to learning about time, this BBC website is helpful for background reading:

www.bbc.co.uk/tiny-happy-people/articles/z3g3cxs
www.ncetm.org.uk/classroom-resources/ey-measures/

SECTION 2 – TASKS

These tasks explore measures.

OUTDOOR TASKS FOR YOUNGER CHILDREN

TASK: BUILD A TOWER

Figure 4.4   Building a tyre tower

PROVIDE

This task can take place outside, with bricks, boxes, tyres, etc., as well as inside with smaller scale blocks. Invite each child to choose what they are going to use. Usually, the younger the child the keener they are on knocking down a tower before it gets too tall. So, rather than the child building one, you may choose to be the builder initially, gradually collaborating on adding blocks. You can use this as an opportunity to narrate what you are doing, using a range of vocabulary to comment on its height and stability: e.g. *taller, high, strong, wider, solid, thick, towering, sturdy, unsteady, stable.*

THE MATHS

This task, which focuses on measuring *height,* can become a favourite and is a perfect context for extending children's comparative vocabulary over time into: e.g. *taller than, shorter than, nearly as tall as,* etc. Comparing the height of towers, either in two different places or on two different occasions, becomes a problem to discuss together and to try to solve. Unless they are alongside one another, the children will have to use an *indirect* method to compare the heights. This is a sophisticated task and involves being able to reason – not necessarily verbally: *"This tower is taller than me, and if that one is shorter than me, it must be the shortest"*. The younger the child the more likely they are to use themselves (and you can use yourself!) to compare to the tower: *"It is lots shorter than you"*, *"It is nearly as tall as me"*. Eventually, with time, you may be able to invite them to build a tower as tall as something else nearby.

WHAT WE DO AND SAY

How will you start, I wonder? Oooo, how high will that be?!

It looks like you are starting with those bricks upright.

I wonder if we can collect enough bricks to make this tower taller than you.

BROADENING THIS OUT

- Collect sticks and make a long line to compare *lengths*, either collaboratively to begin with, or later, individually. If you are working individually and you all begin at the same place, all the lines can be compared directly with one another, and it often becomes a race to be the 'longest'! It is interesting to observe how children choose the sticks. Are they paying attention to their lengths or going for quantity?
- Fill a squeezy bottle with dry sand or similar, making a small hole in the bottom. Children see how far they can walk before the sand runs out, to discuss *length* and *distance*.
- I wonder if ... you can build a tower *exactly as tall as* ....?
- Build towers using a wide selection of blocks so that the children will also be selecting blocks that are good for building, according to their *properties* (shape and space).

Figure 4.5   Building a tower of blocks

TASK: POOH STICKS

PROVIDE

A bridge over some moving water! Sticks the children collect. This is a game that Pooh Bear and Piglet enjoyed playing (A. A. Milne, 1928, *The House at Pooh Corner*).

Children drop their chosen stick into the water from one side of the bridge and see which stick appears, and when, on the other side of the bridge. Encourage them to choose their stick with thought (this is worth observing).

THE MATHS

This task is focused on time and speed. When you play, you will be using time and duration vocabulary, such as *first, next, last, fast, slower, before, then, etc.* You will also be using comparative language to describe the sticks, such as *longer, thicker,* etc.

Children can also be encouraged to think about why a stick may be the best one to appear first or travel faster, or even how to have a *fair* race.

WHAT WE DO AND SAY

Oh look! Mine is first this time!

Is that your stick? How do you know? Are you sure?

You've chosen a longer, fatter stick this time. I wonder why?

Mine is taking ages to come out the other side.

BROADENING THIS OUT

Figure 4.6   Guttering

- If no stream or bridge is available, you can run water along propped up guttering, covering part of the guttering to make a tunnel that small floating objects can disappear into and out of. Placing two lengths of guttering alongside one another can lead to a race. By changing the pitch of the guttering, children can explore *"What happens if ..."*.
- Toy cars can be raced down slopes to see how *far* they travel on steeper or longer slopes.

TASK: FEEDING BIRDS

PROVIDE

A variety of containers for birds to feed from and bird seed. As children choose a container to fill up with bird seed, you can chat about their choice – which one will hold *more or less* food, etc. Once the feeders are hung up, over time you can notice which containers empty first or take longest to empty and discuss why the children think that might be.

THE MATHS

The main aim of this activity is to develop the language of comparison in relation to capacity: *full(er), fill, nearly, enough, height, tall(er) (short(er)), wide(er) (narrow(er)), holds more/less. It can also be an opportunity to begin* to think about comparing containers. Something to observe is whether children notice and comment on the visible differences in shape or size of the containers provided. Can they begin to think about how much the containers can hold (*lots, not much*) and how heavy they feel?

   When the bird feeders are hung, it also stimulates discussions about periods of time as you compare how long it takes for different feeders to empty.

WHAT WE DO AND SAY

I think if we use this large one, it will feed more birds and stay fuller for longer.

This is a heavy one – feel it!

Let's try to stop pouring it in just before it is full so we can fit the lid on.

So, do you think these are the same size?

Which containers do you think the birds (will) like best to use?

(Continued)

BROADENING THIS OUT

- Provide a sack of bird seed and a variety of containers for children to explore filling and emptying.
- Choose and fill containers to hold water for birds to drink from.
- Make pinecone fat balls. Mix room-temperature suet or lard with bird seed and squeeze the mixture into a pinecone tied with twine so you can hang it up. Refrigerate the fat balls before hanging them out. Discuss with the children: "*How long for? How heavy does this one feel?*"
- Directly compare the capacity of two containers by pouring seed from one container into the other one. What can we say about what we see?

TASK: SANDY SOCKS

Figure 4.7   Filling socks

PROVIDE

A selection of old socks in the sandpit, fill them with sand and tie off the tops. You may like to include a child-size wheelbarrow or doll's pushchair to transport the socks, along with some empty socks for them to try to fill. How far can the children carry the socks? Are they too heavy to lift?

Figure 4.8   Heavy socks

THE MATHS

Comparing and understanding weights often begins with experiencing what *heavy, heavier* and *heaviest* mean. Young children are often interested in trying to move something heavy and the sand pit is a perfect place to try this activity.

This task focuses on how children *feel* weight and how they describe it. They can compare socks of sand and decide which they think is heavier/heaviest. You can also begin to help them understand *lighter,* which can be harder to understand, by gradually emptying the sock or bag of sand bit-by-bit and have them feel this each time some sand is removed.

Over time, you may want to introduce some balance scales for children to experience, although they can be difficult for children to fully understand, as the weight on one side of the scale appears to alter as we change what we place on the opposite side.

WHAT WE DO AND SAY

Wow! That one is very heavy – let's see if we can lift it higher/together.

What about this long one – is it as heavy as that one?

(Continued)

I'm filling this bag up now ... heavier, heavier, heavier – I am going to need some help here!

Let's see if we can carry it all the way over there.

BROADENING THIS OUT

- Take this task indoors and put spoons and ankle socks in the sand tray, along with a set of pan-scales to play with.
- Fill balloons with water or old pillowcases with sand, earth or potatoes.
- Look at and feel the weight of vegetables and fruit by putting them into shopping bags and carrying them.

OUTDOOR TASKS FOR OLDER, MORE EXPERIENCED CHILDREN

TASK: BALL RUN

PROVIDE

A selection of guttering, tennis balls or similar items. Chairs, benches, tyres, crates etc. can be used to prop up the guttering. Children construct a journey for their ball using the guttering. Can they make it roll a long way? For a long time?

THE MATHS

This task combines distance, time and speed:

Distance: how *far* they can make their ball travel.

Time: how *long* their ball rolls for.

Speed: how *fast* it travels.

It is often difficult for children to distinguish between these three ideas when they talk about what they notice; they use *fast* or *first* to describe them all. There is also an interesting inverse relationship between speed and time, in that the *slower* the ball rolls, it is more likely it will travel *for a longer period of time* (but not necessarily *further*!). While playing alongside the children, you can clarify their language and support their understanding of these three – complex – ideas and how they interact. Initially, children may be more interested in how *fast* they can make their ball travel down the slope of the guttering and in exploring tipping it more, or less, steeply to change the ball's speed.

After a while, by drawing a 'finishing line' a way off, you can invite children to try to make the ball travel *further*. Trying to keep the ball in motion for longer and comparing times in motion is a more difficult concept to explore and to measure.

This free ramp play booklet (https://youngmindsbigmaths.co.uk/ramp_play/) is a fascinating insight into exploring maths through playing with ramps. It contains examples of children's play, reflections from practitioners, insight from mathematicians and practical advice.

WHAT WE DO AND SAY

What happened?!

Your ball travelled a long way that time.

What shall we try? How about tipping up the first piece of guttering?

Let's have a ball-race.

BROADENING THIS OUT

- Play with a commercial marble run, if available, and then collaborate in making a run for marbles using card, tape, tubing, etc.
- Introduce a sand timer to time the ball's route. Which finishes first? How can we make the ball's run *last longer* than the timer?
- Experiment how to roll toy cars further and further.

TASK: MAGIC POTION

Figure 4.9   Mixing a magic potion

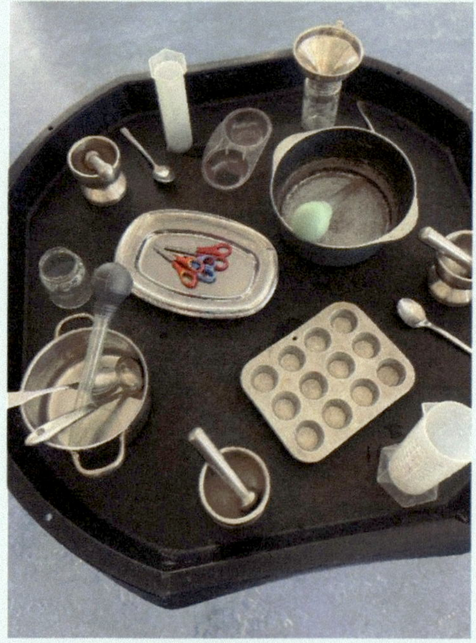

Figure 4.10   Resources for mixing

PROVIDE

A selection of pots, bowls, pouring jugs, jars and containers, pans, spoons, ladles and droppers, coloured water, sand, mud or earth. Later add pebbles and shells, mini-white boards and pens, chalk board and chalks.

Read (or watch on YouTube) Meg and Mog – *Meg's Hiccups* or *A Witch's Spell Party.* Give each child their 'cauldron' and invite them to make a magic potion of their own ("*I wonder what it is for?*"). Gradually, they can be invited to write their recipes (in their own ways) to share.

THE MATHS

This task can be used to develop language and vocabulary related to measuring and comparing amounts (capacity): *more than, less than, fill/full, a small amount, a lot, some more, a lot more, nearly enough, a few drops, a small number of,* etc.

By providing shells or pebbles, for example, as well as small spoons, there are opportunities to do some counting.

At first, children will enjoy mixing and pouring all the 'ingredients', and gradually they can be encouraged to decide what they are going to use to make their potion and to add different amounts of sand, water, pebbles, etc.

WHAT WE DO AND SAY

It's overflowing! Too full!

Oh, this is hard to stir – I need to pour in a little more water.

What will you put in your potion first?

How many spoonfuls?

BROADENING THIS OUT

- Make mud pies or do some pretend baking in the mud kitchen. Provide bun-trays and try to mix the perfect consistency for mud-buns.
- Collaboratively, write a mud-cake recipe which is put in the mud kitchen or sand area to follow and replicate. For those children who are not yet confident writing or reading, use pictures.

TASK: SHADOWS

Figure 4.11   Our shadows hold hands

PROVIDE

You'll need a sunny day! Using playground chalk or a stick to draw in mud or sand, look at shadows at different times of the day. "When are they longer? Shorter? How can we make our shadows wave? … hold hands?"

THE MATHS

This task presents an opportunity to discuss and compare *sizes, lengths and widths,* both between shadows and over time. You can extend vocabulary to *nearer* and *further, taller than, wider than, narrower than,* for example. Shadows also present opportunities to discuss the passage of *time* as well as to explore and describe similarities and differences between the *shapes* of various shadows.

WHAT WE DO AND SAY

Is your shadow taller than/as tall as … you?

Let's draw around your shadow …

I wonder what happens if you lie down in your shadow?

Can you catch your shadow? Your friend's shadow?

BROADENING THIS OUT

- Draw around the shadows of different items. Discuss the shapes. Go out later and see if you can still 'fit' the item inside the outline.
- Make shadows on a wall using a torch indoors. Can we identify the item from its shadow?
- Store blocks by their 'shadows', i.e. draw around the base of the different shaped blocks.

TASK: SQUIRTING WATER

PROVIDE

A collection of washing-up liquid bottles, syringes, etc. After getting themselves and each other thoroughly soaked (!), children see how *far* they can squirt water and, if a wall is available, how *high*. Which squirter makes water travel the *furthest/highest*? Can you reach a set target with every squirter?

THE MATHS

This activity leads to discussions about *length, distance* (*how far*) and *height,* and to making comparisons between them. Children can make a direct comparison if they stand in the same place and squirt together, but to begin with they will enjoy squirting and running to see where each squirt lands. Does it make a difference how *full* the bottle is? If we stand *higher* on a step or block?

We can extend our children's understanding of measures by inviting them to consider comparisons, by using 'as' and 'than'. For example: *nearly as long/high as, just a little shorter/longer than, about the same distance as, etc.* Eventually, you can consider drawing a chalk line to stand at, with children marking where they squirt to each time.

WHAT WE DO AND SAY

I think this will be the best squirter ... do you think it will travel the furthest?

I am going to squirt mine to land as tall as I think you are on that wall, then we can check how close I am.

(Continued)

Figure 4.12   Squirting water high

Figure 4.13   Squirting water far

That's the furthest of all of us!

What about this squirter? What do you think?

I wonder where you can stand so you don't get wet!

BROADENING THIS OUT

- Squirt a required length – measure out a metre and see if you can land *nearly* or *exactly* on the metre line. What about trying a short length? Or squirting how tall you are?
- Squirt a water picture. Can you make your squirter last until your picture is finished?
- See how *long* it takes for different squirters to empty (time).
- Compare how much water different squirters hold (capacity).

INDOOR TASKS FOR YOUNGER CHILDREN

TASK: FITTING IN

Figure 4.14   Nesting boxes

Figure 4.15   Tower of boxes

PROVIDE

Items and toys that nest, e.g. stacking bath cups, dolls, display baskets. Some of them can have lids, which is extra useful, and some will stack to make a tower.

An alternative is to provide a range of differently sized plastic, lidded containers for children to match up.

THE MATHS

This task combines elements of shape with comparative sizes (measures). To 'nest' items successfully, children have to pay attention to the size, position and shape of the stacking toys. Being able to fit an item successfully into a space involves us visualising both its size and how we may need to flip or turn it (spatial visualisation). Children use trial and improvement to do this to begin with, but you can begin to ask them to think about how something might fit before they try. Observing a child take a nesting set apart and then fit it together again, leaving none out, will tell you a lot about how much attention they are paying to the relative size of the items in the set. Playing with these toys over and over will help children to become more accurate in selecting the correct item, or the correct lid for each box, for example. As well as the language of size – *too big, just right,*

(Continued)

fits, etc. – this task also focuses on *ordinal* aspects, such as *first, next, after, before,* and spatial language, such as *turn* and *twist.*

WHAT WE DO AND SAY

Let's play with these.

I wonder which one fits in next? That fits just right!

Oh, this one is left out!

Let's try using them all to build a tower ... you find the biggest one for the bottom.

Let's see ... do they all have lids, I wonder?

BROADENING THIS OUT

- If you can get hold of some large boxes, children can explore which ones they can fit into. Or build some hidey-holes of different sizes for children to squeeze into.
- When children are very familiar with a set of stacking cups, put the set out with one piece missing. Will they spot the missing piece?
- Filling bags and boxes. Provide gift bags and or gift boxes of varying sizes and create a simple 'shop' where items have to be packed into an appropriately sized bag or box.

TASK: PHOTO SORT

PROVIDE

Access to photographs on a smartphone or a tablet, or hard copies, which must be of relevance to the children – they can be taken of them in your setting, engaging in tasks they enjoy. This is an ideal activity to engage in with families. If using hard copies, lay them out on a plain tablecloth or blanket on the floor for easy access, or display a selection on a tablet or interactive whiteboard (IWB). You can begin by drawing a child's attention to one or two of the photographs and commenting on them.

THE MATHS

Children start to grasp time concepts around the age of 2, and it begins with their understanding of the past, rather than anything in the future. This is because the past relies on us using our memories, which we can share. Photographs, however they are stored, are an ideal way to explore the concept of time, both over longer periods of time and to review a day's outing or event. Useful language to use includes: *remember, long while ago, last week, yesterday, afternoon/morning, winter/spring etc., first, next, before, after, then.* Selecting one photograph from each month of the year to create a timeline of the school year, month by month, displayed where families can see it, stimulates lots of discussion throughout the year.

WHAT WE DO AND SAY

I remember this. We were outside making mud pies!

This was last time we went to the park, do you remember...?

Can you find a photo you like – what were you doing then?

Oh look! There are you and Josh on the climbing frame – that was last week.

Can we put these photos in order? What did we do first?

BROADENING THIS OUT

- Look at photos from a long time ago when the child was younger, or when members of their family were children, and compare these images to today's photos. This activity needs to be approached with sensitivity to differing family situations.
- Invite the child to find photos of what they like doing and relate this image to what they might do in the future. For example, "You loved splashing in the paddling pool, didn't you? When the weather is warmer, in the summer, you can do that again."
- If there is an event you are looking forward to, display a picture of this and introduce a visible countdown of days.

TASK: BALLOON RISING

PROVIDE

A helium-filled balloon on a long piece of ribbon, hidden in a pillowcase or something similar. This task works best in a high-ceilinged room.

Remove the balloon from the bag, making sure everyone is *"Looking, looking, looking ..."*. Build up the excitement! Gradually let out the ribbon so the balloon climbs higher and higher. Stop before it reaches the ceiling. 'Walk' the balloon around the room. Continue to let out the ribbon. Wonder aloud if it will touch the ceiling, and whether you will be able to reach it to get it down again. Pull it down and up to encourage comments.

An outdoors alternative can be to throw a rope attached to a bucket or basket over the branch of a tree and pull it up and down.

THE MATHS

The main aim of this playful activity is to interest children in comparing height and to contextualise language to do with height and distance: *higher than, as high as, low down, lower, high up, further, up/down, near(er), far, distance, nearly reach*, etc. As children hear these words, they begin to understand how to use them themselves. There is a link here to the positional and directional language we use, such as *up, down, above, below.*

WHAT WE DO AND SAY

Oooo I think it might touch the ceiling...

It's as high as the window.

It's going up, up, up....

The ribbon is running out! I don't have much to hold on to.

What if I let go of the ribbon ...?

Can I reach the ribbon do you think?

How can I get the balloon down?

BROADENING THIS OUT

- Leave the balloon for children to pull down and let back up. Maybe use differently shaped balloons to explore and compare heights.
- One day, make the ribbon too short to reach and ask for suggestions on how to solve the problem of getting the balloon back!

- Give each child a sticky dot and ask them to stretch up as high as they can to stick the dot on a wall. Compare how high the children can reach by comparing the dots and who can reach the *furthest* as well as the *highest*.

INDOOR TASKS FOR OLDER, MORE EXPERIENCED CHILDREN

TASK: ICE CUBES

Figure 4.16   Ice cubes

PROVIDE

Ice cube tray and containers of coloured water. Start by filling the ice cube trays with coloured water together and freezing them.

Once frozen, tip the ice cubes into transparent bowls or on to trays and leave them for children to observe what happens.

(Continued)

THE MATHS

This task is aimed at stimulating discussion about *size* and about *time* and *how long* it takes for the ice to freeze and then to melt: *soon, later, before/after, slower, faster, tomorrow, hours, etc.* You can talk about what affects this transformation, as well as discuss *size, number* and *quantity: smaller than, fewer than,* etc.

WHAT WE DO AND SAY

We'll put these in our freezer until this afternoon. I wonder if that's enough time for them to be frozen?

I'm not sure if they are frozen yet … How can we tell?

I wonder where we can put them so they melt fastest?

How long will it take the ice cubes to melt? How can we time it?

Oh, that's de-frosted faster! Look how small these cubes are now.

BROADENING THIS OUT

- Ask the children: "Shall we put some in the fridge/outside to see if they freeze?"
- Put bowls of ice cubes in different places to melt and compare times, e.g. on a radiator, pouring water over them, etc.
- If you have clock timers or a timer on a smartphone, discuss the numbers on clock timers and watch the countdown on a digital timer.

TASK: MAKE A LIST

PROVIDE

To begin, regularly chat about a few key things that are going to happen that day, ticking these off on your fingers, e.g. "First we're going upstairs to clean our teeth and then, when we're ready, we'll get in the buggy and catch the bus to the shops. After that we'll go to the swings on the way home."

When you feel it is appropriate, provide long, narrow sheets of paper on clipboards (or stiff card with pegs) and pens. Collaboratively, make a simple *'To do'* list of the different things that children might do that morning.

Figure 4.17   'To do' list

Encourage children to tick or cross out what they do as they do it. The list can be discussed afterwards: "What did they do *first/next?* What did they spend *longer* doing?"

Children may like to begin to make their own lists, which may or may not match what they actually do!

Figure 4.18   Child's list

(Continued)

THE MATHS

This task is focused on ordering events and beginning to understand the *passing of time.* Children can begin to understand this concept if we relate time passing to familiar activities, ordering them *first, next, then, after, before,* and beginning to think about which *took more or less time.*

WHAT WE DO AND SAY

What are we going to play with today? I am going to write a list here.

What three things will you do this morning, Amar?

I think you might start with the bikes first, Sophie.

Let's look at what you've all ticked this morning.

Did you play with the blocks? When was that?

BROADENING THIS OUT

- Some older children may be interested in looking at one month on a calendar (either as hard copy or on a tablet) and writing in what is going to happen on particular days.
- Read together *'The List',* in Arnold Lobel's *Frog and Toad Together.* www.youtube.com/watch?v=uiu-WATnk7A. *'The Garden',* in the same book, is also about time passing.
- Gradually, children may become interested in placing a sand timer alongside their chosen task to see how long the task lasts (i.e. how many times you turn the timer over).

TASK: PLAYDOUGH BALLS

Figure 4.19   Playdough ball

PROVIDE

Playdough and more than one set of pan-balances, cutting tools and bun trays. Invite children to roll balls (buns) to fit in the bun trays and weigh in the pan-balances.

THE MATHS

The focus of this task is developing young children's interest in *size* and *weight* (mass). Pan-balances only allow two weights to be compared directly. Ordering the weights of more than two playdough balls requires a sophisticated ability to replace one for another and thought processes such as: "*If* A is heavier than B, and B is heavier than C, *then* C is the lightest." We wouldn't expect a child under age 7 to be able to think abstractly like this, thus, ordering items by weight is challenging. Focusing on fostering and progressing children's understanding of weight-specific, comparative language (*heavier/lighter than, lightest, a little heavier than, just about the same weight …*), and beginning to consider accuracy by looking at the concept of *the same weight* using *balance*, is important.

Making playdough balls for the bun tray will also provide opportunities for *number-talk*, looking at how many bun spaces are filled, how many are left, etc.

(Continued)

WHAT WE DO AND SAY

Let's make some buns for the bun tray. What flavours will yours be?

You've rolled a big ball! Let's weigh it like this.

I'm going to put my bun in this side. Let's see if your bun is heavier – how will we know?

What do you think/see?

Oooo, I've made the scales balance … these playdough balls must be the same weight. Now you have a go.

BROADENING THIS OUT

- Introduce some gram weights to use when weighing. It may be easier for children to understand what is happening if the scales have one pan for the playdough balls opposite one flat place for the weights (kitchen scales).

Figure 4.20   Kitchen scales

- Make some elastic weighing 'machines' to compare more than two things. You will need the bottom cut from juice containers, made into a small basket with string, suspended by an elastic band and attached to a wall.
- As you drop different items into each juice-basket (potato, orange, etc.), it will drop a certain amount. This is a rudimentary spring balance and, if using more than two, it allows for more than two items to be compared by weight.

Figure 4.21   Elastic scales

- Lift and compare carrier bags holding potatoes.
- Roll playdough worms and compare their lengths.

SECTION 3 – PICTURE BOOKS

Banyai, I. (1995). *Zoom*. A wordless picture book that zooms out from a farm, to a child playing with a farm set, to a magazine picture, and so on, ending up with an image of the world in space. Mind-blowing!

Cronin, D., & Bliss, H. (2003). *Diary of a Worm*. A worm keeps a dated journal through the summer months.

Hoban, T. (1985). *Is it larger? Is It smaller?* A wordless book of photographs comparing the sizes of many different familiar and not so familiar items. Lots to discuss.

Leedy, L. (2000). *Measuring Penny*. Penny, a Boston Terrier, is measured for a homework project. Measuring is explained. A mixture of imperial and metric measures are explored.

Limenrtani, A. (2017). *How Long is a Whale?* A factual book comparing the length of a whale to 10 sea otters, 9 yellowfin tuna, 8 sealions, and so on, including the lengths of the different sea creatures in metres.

Stoll Walsh, E. (2010). *Balancing Act*. Two mice use a stick and a rock to make a see-saw and different friends help them to balance.

RHYMES AND SONGS

(Using one finger on each hand for each blackbird, make them appear and disappear from behind your back with the following words.)

Two little blackbirds sitting on a hill
One named Jack, one named Jill
Fly away Jack, fly away Jill
Come back Jack, come back Jill.

(In the flowing verses, act out the vocabulary – High and Low, Fast and Slow, etc. – in each verse.)

Two little blackbirds flying in the sky
One named Low, one named High
Fly away Low, fly away High
Come back Low, come back High

Two little blackbirds sitting on a pole
One named Fast, one named Slooow
Fly away Fast, fly away Slooow
Come back Fast, come back Slooow

Two little blackbirds sitting on a gate
One named Early, one named Late
Fly away Early, fly away Late
Come back Early, come back Late.

Figure 5.0 Children and sticks

5

SOME CONCLUDING REMARKS

This book is an invitation for you to be playful with mathematics. At its root are the following principles: that mathematics can and should be engaging, child-led, based in play and prioritise joint communication, exploration, challenge and joy, with adults and children learning together in a supportive, positive environment. We can (and should) positively influence our children's attitude to mathematics by how we are and how we behave. Mathematics and being mathematical is something that resides in all of us, including young children, rather than on paper or on a screen, and it is our job to draw children's attention to this and to draw it out.

> *"From birth, children in all cultures develop in physical environments containing a multitude of objects and events that can support mathematics learning in everyday life (Ginsburg & Seo, 1999). A large number of parallel bars on the side of babies' cribs; stalks of corn in a field are similarly arranged in rows; there is a larger number of candies or stones in one collection than other; the toy is under the chair, not on top of it; blocks can be cubes and balls are spheres; in the field, one cow is front of the tree and another behind it. Although varying in many ways, including the availability of books, schools and 'educational' toys, all environments surely contain objects to count, shapes to discriminate, and locations to identify. The objects and events are not themselves mathematics, but they afford mathematical thinking."*
>
> (Ginsburg 2009:146)

The key that unlocks these affordances, in the above paragraph, is the adult, sensitively drawing children's attention to what they notice, create and what they can do.

On occasions, I, and others working in early years, have been asked for a mathematics 'programme' or mathematics scheme for nursery-aged children. This is a sad reflection of where we are in the first quarter of the 21st century. Working effectively mathematically with children does not require the purchase of a scheme or a series of workbooks. Working effectively mathematically with children *does* require adults who are both knowledgeable and confident, and who enjoy playing mathematically with their children. Both this book and my

Figure 5.1   Adult and children playing mathematically

companion book for those working with 3- to 7-year-old children (Williams 2022) have been written to support all adults, in families, pre-school settings, nurseries and reception classes, in becoming more confident and knowledgeable, whatever their own mathematical background and experience. Those of us working in early years bring our own unique talents to the job and often share core values, which include an empathetic, playful, nurturing approach to our teaching. This book has been written to remind us that approaching mathematics is no different.

I hope the activities in this book emphasise the everyday-ness of mathematics and that what is most important for young children's mathematical development is the conversations we have together, drawing out their thinking, such as: *"Ooo, that's interesting, I wonder if that will fit inside?"*, or *"What shall we try now?"*. These to-and-fro interactions are known as 'sustained shared thinking' in early years' literature (Sylva et al. 2004), where this two-way process of speaking and listening was pinpointed as central to supporting children's deep learning. We don't need to be afraid of the language, of getting something 'wrong', or of not knowing an answer, as we create situations where children's mathematical curiosity and creativity can flourish. Instead, we can ponder with them: *"I have no idea about that. Let's try*

Figure 5.2   Lifting a pumpkin

something and see", and encourage them to try out their ideas. As we increase our awareness of the mathematical potential of everyday activities, such as doing the washing (*"How many? Which matches? Enough space? … "*), eating our meals *("We need four plates and the same number of cups. Are there enough? Too many? … ")* and playing *("Can we use all the same bricks? Will this fit? … "),* our mathematical interactions will increase. It stands to reason that the more we talk about maths the more our children learn about maths.

Finally, the four statutory overarching principles of the *English Early Years Foundation Stage* (Department for Education 2024a, 2024b) apply to *mathematics* learning and teaching as to every other area of learning:

- Every child is **a unique child**, who is constantly learning and who can be resilient, capable, confident and self-assured (*mathematically, with the support of positive, playful adults*).
- Children learn to be strong and independent through **positive relationships** (*with the substance of mathematics as well as with peers and adults*).
- Children learn and develop well in **enabling environments** with teaching and support from adults, who respond to their individual interests and needs and help them to build their learning over time (*who are offered mathematics aligned with what they are already doing and interested in, with time to play with new ideas and re-visit activities*).

- The importance of **learning and development**. Children develop and learn at different rates *(children's mathematical development is broad – as in every other area – and has more in common with different paths taken from one point to another, than a straight line of progression that is the same for every child)*.

If we are being asked to adhere to one scheme of work, or to fit into a mathematics programme that is being used in the later years of education in order that we prepare children adequately for the next stage, we need to hold onto these four principles and remind people of them. We need to remind ourselves that the best preparation for later learning is doing what is appropriate, now.

Figure 5.3 Fitting balls into boxes

Julian is an experienced and exciting nursery teacher. Recently he spoke to me about his own development from a teacher who made children do things to a teacher who provided things that children wanted to do. My hope is that we can all make a similar switch, mathematically, for our children. That, with the help of this book, practitioners believe in playful mathematics and feel empowered to have a go in supporting it. Our mission is to find out what children like to do, what mathematics may be happening almost naturally and, with our 'maths play' hats on, enhance it mathematically through intentional play.

I leave the last words to a 3-year-old talking to the driver from the back seat of a car. How might you playfully follow up a conversation like this?

Sam:	Am I on the left side? Which side am I on?
Adult:	Yes, the left side.
Sam:	And is Alice on the right side?
Adult:	Yes.
Sam:	And are you on the right side?
Adult:	Yes.
Sam:	And is this belt [indicating the empty front left passenger seat] on the left side?
Adult:	Yes, that's right. (sic!)
[Pause]	
Sam:	When we turn round in a minute I'll be on the right side.

REFERENCES

Baratta-Lorton, M. (1976). *Mathematics their way.* Addison-Wesley.

Cahoon, A., Gilmore, C., & Simms, V. (2021). Developmental pathways of early numerical skills during the preschool to school transition. *Learning and Instruction, 75,* 1–14.

Catling, S. (2005). Children's understanding of maps: Implications for teaching mapping skills. In C. Lee & C. Chew Hung (Eds.), *Primary social studies: Exploring pedagogy and content* (pp. 74–98). Marshall Cavendish International.

Cheng, Y.-L., & Mix, K. S. (2014). Spatial training improves children's mathematics ability. *Journal of Cognition and Development, 15*(1), 2–11. https://doi.org/10.1080/15248372.2012.725186

Clements, D. H., & Sarama, J. (2021). *Learning and teaching early math: The learning trajectories approach* (3rd ed.). Routledge.

Cuoco, A., Goldenberg, E. P., & Mark, J. (1996). Habits of mind: An organizing principle for mathematics curricula. *Journal of Mathematical Behavior, 15,* 375–402.

Department for Education. (2024a). *Statutory framework for the foundation stage, for group and school-based providers.* Crown Copyright. www.gov.uk/government/publications/early-years-foundation-stage-framework--2

Department for Education. (2024b). *Statutory framework for the foundation stage, for childminders.* Crown Copyright. www.gov.uk/government/publications/early-years-foundation-stage-framework--2

Dindyal, J. (2015). Geometry in the early years: A commentary. *ZDM Mathematics Education, 47,* 519–529.

Dowker, A., Cheriton, O., Horton, R., & Mark, W. (2019). Relationships between attitudes and performance in English and Chinese first-grade children's mathematics. *Educational Studies in Mathematics, 100*(3).

Duncan, G. J., Dowcett, C., Claessens, A., & Magnuson, K. (2007). School readiness and later achievement. *Developmental Psychology, 43*(6), 1428–1446. https://doi.org/10.1037/0012-1649.43.6.1428

Farran, E. K., McCarthy, S., Gilligan-Lee, K. A., Bates, K. E., & Gripton, C. (2024). Translating research to practice: Practitioner use of the spatial reasoning toolkit. *Gifted Child Today, 47*(3), 202–215.

Gifford, S. (2018). Subitising. *nrich,* 23 October. https://nrich.maths.org/articles/subitising

Gifford, S., Gripton, C., Williams, H. J., Lancaster, A., Bates, K. E., Williams, A. Y., Gilligan-Lee, K., Borthwick, A., & Farran, E. K. (2022). *Spatial reasoning in early childhood.* https://psyarxiv.com/jnwpu/download?format=pdf

Gilligan, K. A., Hodgkiss, A., Thomas, M. S., & Farran, E. K. (2019). The developmental relations between spatial cognition and mathematics in primary school children. *Developmental Science, 22*(4) https://doi.org/10.1111/desc.12786

Ginsburg, H. G. (2009). Mathematical play and playful mathematics: A guide for early education. In D. Singer, R. Golinkoff, & K. Hirsh-Pasek (Eds.), *Play = Learning: How play motivates and enhances children's cognitive and social-emotional growth.* Oxford University Press.

Gripton, C. (2022). Pattern in the early years mathematics curriculum: A 25-year review of the status, positioning and conception of pattern in England. *Research in Mathematics Education, 25*(1), 3–23.

Gripton, C., & Williams, H. J. (2023). The principles for appropriate pedagogy in early mathematics: Exploration, apprenticeship and sense-making. *Chartered College: A research review.* https://my.chartered.college/early-childhood-hub/the-principles-for-appropriate-pedagogy-in-early-mathematics-exploration-apprenticeship-and-sense-making/

Gussin Paley, V. (1981). *Wally's stories: Conversations in the kindergarten.* Harvard University Press.

Levine, S. C., Goldin-Meadow, S., Carlson, M. T., & Hemani-Lopez, N. (2018). Mental transformation skill in young children: The role of concrete and abstract motor training. *Cognitive Science, 42*, 1207–1228.

Malaguzzi, L. (2012). 'No way the hundred is there'. In C. Edwards, L. Gandini & G. Forman (eds.), *The hundred languages of children: The Reggio Emilia experience in transformation,* 3rd edn. ABC-CLIO.

Mason, J., Burton, L., & Stacey, K. (2010). *Thinking mathematically.* Pearson.

Mercer, N., & Hodgkinson, S. (Eds.). (2008). *Exploring talk in school: Inspired by the work of Douglas Barnes.* Sage.

Mulligan, J., & Mitchelmore, M. (2009). Awareness of pattern and structure in early mathematical development. *Mathematics Education Research Journal, 21*(2), 33–49.

Mulligan, J., Oslington, G., & English, L. (2020). Supporting early mathematical development through a 'pattern and structure' intervention program. *ZDM Mathematics Education, 52*, 663–676.

Nunes, T., & Bryant, P. (2009). *Key understandings in mathematics learning:Paper 2 Understanding whole numbers. A review commissioned by the Nuffield Foundation.* Nuffield Foundation.

Obersteiner, A. (2019). Multiple pathways between affect and mathematical competence in young children. *Educational Studies in Mathematics, 100*(3), 317–323.

Papic, M., & Mulligan, J. (2007). The growth of early mathematical patterning: An intervention study. *Proceedings of the 30th Annual Conference of the Mathematics Education Research Group of Australasia, 2*, 591–600.

Pritulsky, C., Murano, C., Odean, R., Bower, C., Hirsh-Patek, K., & Golinkoff, R. M. (2020). Spatial thinking: Why it belongs in the preschool classroom. *Translational Issues in Psychological Science, 6*(3), 271–282.

Reikeras, E. (2020). Relations between play skills and mathematical skills in toddlers. *ZDM Mathematics Education, 52*, 703–716. https://doi.org/10.1007/s11858-020-01141-1

Sarama, J., Clements, D. H., Barrett, J. E., Cullen, C. J., Hudyma, A., & Vanegas, Y. (2021). Length measurement in the early years: Teaching and learning with learning trajectories. *Mathematical Thinking and Learning, 24*(4), 267–290. https://doi.org/10.1080/10986065.2020.1858245

Schoenfeld, A. H. (1992). Learning to think mathematically: Problem solving, metacognition and sense making in mathematics. In D. A. Grows (Ed.), *Handbook of research on mathematics teaching and learning* (pp. 334–370). Macmillan.

Skene, K., O'Farrelly, C. M., Byrne, E. M., Kirby, N., Stevens, E. C., & Ramchandani, P. G. (2022). Can guidance during play enhance children's learning and development in educational contexts? A systematic review and meta-analysis. *Child Development, 93*(4), 1162–1180. doi: 10.1111/cdev.13730

Sorby, S. A., & Panther, G. C. (2020). Is the key to better PISA math scores improving spatial skills? *Mathematics Education Research Journal, 32*, 213–233.

Su, F. (2020). *Mathematics for human flourishing.* Yale University Press.

Sylva, K., Melhuish, E. C., Sammons, P., Siraj-Blatchford, I., & Taggart, B. (2004). *The Effective Provision of Pre-School Education (EPPE) project: Technical Paper 12 – The final report: Effective pre-school education.* DfES, Institute of Education, University of London.

Szilagyi, J., Sarama, J., & Clements, D. (2013). Young children's understandings of length measurement: Evaluating a learning trajectory. *Journal for Research in Mathematics Education, 44*(3), 581–620. https://doi.org/10.5951/jresematheduc.44.3.0581

Thouless, H., Gifford, S., Moses, K., & James, R. (2020). Reasoning about patterns. *Mathematics Teaching, 271*, 30–34.

Uttal, D. H., Meadow, N. G., Newcombe, N. S., Tipton, E., Hand, L. L., Alden, A. R., & Warren, C. (2013). Malleability of spatial skills: A meta-analysis of training studies. *Psychological Bulletin, 139*(2), 352–402.

Verdine, B. N., Golinko, M., Hirsh-Pasek, K., & Newcombe, N. S. (2017). How early spatial skills predict later spatial and mathematical skills. *Monographs of the Society for Research in Child Development.* https://doi.org/10.1111/mono.12285

Voutsina, C., & Stott, D. (2023). Numbers in everyday life: Fostering children's curiosity about numbers in the world around them (NiEL). https://mathicw.soton.ac.uk/project-2/

Vygotsky, L. S. (1966). Play and its role in the mental development of the child. *Soviet Psychology, 5*(3), 6–18. https://doi.org/10.2753/RPO1061-040505036

Williams, H. J. (2022). *Playful mathematics for children 3 to 7.* Sage.

APPENDIX

VOCABULARY AND LANGUAGE

Vocabulary and language are different and related.

Language is the main method of human communication, consisting of words conveyed by speech, writing and gesture, whereas *vocabulary* is the collection of words used in a particular language. Vocabulary is part of language and language consists of all forms of communication. Importantly for young children, this includes all their many ways of communicating their thoughts and ideas.

Loris Malaguzzi, the early childhood pioneer and founder of the Reggio Emillia pre-schools in Northern Italy is known for coining the phrase "the 100 languages of children" referring to the infinite ways children express themselves to connect their thoughts, feeling and imaginings through opportunities they are given to depict their understandings of the world through drawing, sculpting, dramatic play, writing and painting (Malaguzzi 2012). Mathematically, children of all ages are often only offered a restricted 'language' to respond to mathematics (formal language and written representations), which many find difficult to understand. In engaging with the tasks in this book, I hope you can appreciate how important it is for all children to be invited to, and given the time to, express themselves mathematically using their own words, their drawing and symbolising and gesture. These opportunities will include using their *informal* language and vocabulary alongside hearing and beginning to use formal mathematical vocabulary. For example, *roundy* as well as *circle* or *pointy* as well as *triangle*.

In what follows, **mathematical conversations** collate some adult contributions that are useful for fostering children's mathematical language and thinking. At this age, we may not receive many replies to our questions, but it is important to begin to draw children's attention to the thinking we value by asking the questions. It is also important for us to remember that, particularly when working with toddlers and the youngest children, statements and 'ponderings' are less intrusive and often open up more conversations than direct questions – e.g. *"I see you are picking out all the longer blocks than this one"*, or

"Hmmm, I am wondering why you are choosing those longer blocks" – as opposed to *"Is this block longer or shorter than this one?"* It is also important to include in some of our questions words that require a non-verbal response from the child, such as *point to, find me* or *choose.*

Below, I have listed some useful **mathematical vocabulary** that we use under the three areas of 'shape and space', 'number and pattern' and 'measures'. It is not an exhaustive list, but rather an indication of the range we need to be aware of, in order to communicate effectively mathematically.

Much the same as any language learning, we are steeping young children in mathematical language and vocabulary, and at this age, we will be the ones mainly using the formal vocabulary and they will be hearing it. As the children get older, we may hear and see them using some of this vocabulary 'in real time', i.e. by themselves with peers as they play. This usage is exciting and indicates their understanding of those words.

MATHEMATICAL CONVERSATIONS

I wonder what happens if we …

What if I …

Shall we try this now …

Let's try …

Let's remember that we thought …

What do you see? What do you notice?

What do you wonder?

How do you know?

I really want to know more about …

Where have you seen one like this?

I am thinking … what about you?

Do you think …?

I wonder if that is the same?

Ooo, that was tricky! That involved you doing a lot of thinking!

What will you do (differently) tomorrow, do you think?

How can we remember how many?

What comes first … now what …?

Do you have a plan?

What happened?!

How did that go? Would you change anything if you started again?

MATHEMATICAL VOCABULARY

Words and vocabulary for different areas of mathematics.

SHAPE AND SPACE

(Three dimensional) *pyramid, cone, cube, cuboid, sphere, flat face, curved face, straight edge, curved edge, slope, corner, hollow, solid, flat, build, tall(er), construct, balance, symmetrical, similar, different (to), the same as, choose, imagine, shape*

(Two dimensional) *circle, square, rectangle, star, straight line, curved line, side, point, fold, pattern, balance, symmetrical, match, show me, arrange, choose, imagine, same, different, similar*

(Location and direction) *over, under, underneath, above, below, top, bottom, outside, inside, on, in, up, down, around, in front, behind, beside, between, opposite, apart, together, middle, along, across, through, towards, away from, place, hide*

NUMBER AND PATTERN

all the counting numbers, number, nought, zero, none, few, many, more (than), fewer (than), less (than), least, most, lots, a lot more/less/fewer than, count, count backwards, count forwards, count from, every one, every other one, each, compare, put them in order, muddle them up, equal to, the same as, guess, too many/few, about the same (amount), nearly, (not) enough, how many (more), left, left over, most, check, work out, remember, think, start from, join in, missing, one at a time

collect, imagine, start from, choose, pattern, similar to, different from, balance, repeat, copy, carry on, continue, arrange, put, place, similar, different, belongs

MEASURES

(Time) *before, after, day, week, month, hour, minute, birthday, holiday, quick, quicker, quickest, first, second, last, next, how long, takes longer, takes less time, sometimes, always, morning, afternoon, evening, night, list, order, most often, occasionally, seasons, days of the week, months of the year, ages*

(Length and height) *length, height, width, long(er/est), short(er/est), fat(er/est), wide(er/est), narrow(er/est), thick(er/est), thin(er/est), deep(er/est), shallow(er/est), high(er/est) low(er/est), tall(er/est), higher than, further than, lower than, wider than, far, further, near, close, build, make, the same height /length, different height /length*

(Weight) *weight, balance, balances, scales, heavy, heavier/est, light, lighter/est, heavier/ lighter than, the same weight, nearly the same weight, different weights, a little/a lot heavier/lighter than*

(Capacity) *full, empty, emptier, nearly as full as, fuller than, not quite enough, nearly full, too much, holds, container, jug, cupful, spoonful, drop, small amount, large amount, the same amount, a different amount, half full*

INDEX